STUDIO PAPERBACK

Günter Behnisch

Peter Blundell Jones

Birkhäuser – Publishers for Architecture
Basel · Berlin · Boston

Translation English/German:
Nora von Mühlendahl

Translation German/English
(captions, list of buildings):
Susanne Schindler

Redaktionelle Leitung und Layout/
Senior editor and layout:
Christian Kandzia

Redaktion/Editor:
Dagmar Renfranz

A CIP catalogue record for this book is available from the
Library of Congress, Washington, D. C., USA

Die Deutsche Bibliothek – CIP-Einheitsaufnahme

Behnisch, Günter:
Günter Behnisch / Peter Blundell Jones. [Transl. Engl./German: Nora von Mühlendahl.
Transl. German/Engl. (captions, list of buildings): Susanne Schindler]. - Basel ; Boston ; Berlin : Birkhäuser, 2000
  ISBN 3-7643-6046-1

This work is subject to copyright. All rights are reserved, whether the whole or part of the material is concerned, specifically the rights of translation, reprinting, re-use of illustrations, recitation, broadcasting, reproduction on microfilms or in other ways, and storage in data banks. For any kind of use, permission of the copyright owner must be obtained.

© 2000 Birkhäuser – Publishers for Architecture,
P. O. Box 133, CH-4010 Basel, Switzerland
Printed on acid-free paper produced from chlorine-free pulp
Printed in Germany
ISBN 3-7643-6046-1

9 8 7 6 5 4 3 2 1

Inhalt

Contents

7	**Einführung**		7	**Introduction**
25	**Bauten und Projekte**		25	**Buildings and Projects**

	Schulbauten			**Educational Buildings**
26	Hohenstaufen-Gymnasium, Göppingen		26	Hohenstaufen grammar school, Göppingen
28	Vogelsangschule, Stuttgart		28	Vogelsang school, Stuttgart
30	Fachhochschule/Hochschule für Technik, Ulm		30	Ulm engineering school
33	Progymnasium (jetzt Hauptschule), Furtwangen		33	Grammar school (now secondary modern school), Furtwangen
34	Nachbarschaftsschule «In den Berglen», Berglen-Oppelsbohm		34	"In den Berglen" school, Berglen-Oppelsbohm
36	Progymnasium auf dem Schäfersfeld, Lorch		36	Auf dem Schäfersfeld grammar school, Lorch
40	Fritz-Erler-Schule, Pforzheim		40	Fritz Erler school, Pforzheim
44	Bildungszentrum der Evangelischen Landeskirche in Württemberg, Stuttgart-Birkach		44	Seminary Centre of the Württemberg Protestant Church, Stuttgart-Birkach
48	Hauptschule auf dem Schäfersfeld, Lorch		48	Auf dem Schäfersfeld secondary modern school, Lorch
52	Albert-Schweitzer-Sonderschule, Bad Rappenau		52	Albert Schweitzer special school, Bad Rappenau
54	Kaufmännische Schule, Öhringen		54	Business school, Öhringen
58	St. Benno-Gymnasium, Dresden		58	St Benno grammar school, Dresden
	Sportbauten			**Buildings for Sport**
62	Sporthalle, Schwenningen		62	School sports-hall, Schwenningen
63	Turnhalle der Oskar-von-Miller-Realschule, Rothenburg ob der Tauber		63	School sports-hall, Rothenburg ob der Tauber
65	Olympiapark, München		65	Olympic Park, Munich
74	Trainings- und Aufwärmhalle für die Olympiade, München		74	Training and warm-up hall for Munich Olympics
76	Schulsporthalle, Lorch		76	School sports-hall, Lorch
78	Sporthalle, Sindelfingen		78	Sports-hall, Sindelfingen
82	Sporthalle, Sulzbach an der Murr		82	Sports-hall, Sulzbach on Murr
	Sozialbauten			**Social Buildings**
84	Alten- und Pflegeheim, Reutlingen		84	Old people's home and nursing home, Reutlingen
88	Kindergarten, Stuttgart-Neugereut		88	Kindergarten, Stuttgart-Neugereut
90	Kindergarten, Stuttgart-Luginsland		90	Kindergarten, Stuttgart-Luginsland
94	Sozialer Wohnungsbau, Ingolstadt-Hollerstauden		94	Social housing, Ingolstadt-Hollerstauden
97	Umbau und Erweiterung des Kurhauses, Bad Elster		97	Conversion and extension of spa buildings, Bad Elster
101	Hallenbad, Leipzig-Grünau		101	Swimming baths complex, Leipzig-Grünau

	Kulturbauten		**Cultural Buildings**
104	Deutsche Bibliothek, Frankfurt am Main	104	National Library, Frankfurt on Main
106	Hysolar-Institut der Universität Stuttgart, Stuttgart-Vaihingen	106	Hysolar research institute, Stuttgart-Vaihingen
110	Universitätsbibliothek, Eichstätt	110	University library, Eichstätt
114	Museum für Post und Kommunikation, Frankfurt am Main	114	Post and Communications Museum, Frankfurt on Main
119	Akademie der Künste Berlin-Brandenburg, Berlin	119	New building for the Berlin-Brandenburg Arts Academy, Berlin
123	Theater- und Konzerthalle, Bristol	123	Arts centre, Bristol
127	Lothar-Günther-Buchheim-Museum, Bernried	127	Lothar-Günther Buchheim Museum, Bernried
130	Staatsarchiv, Kopenhagen	130	National and Provincial Archives building, Copenhagen
	Verwaltungs- und Industriebauten		**Commercial Buildings**
134	Herbert-Keller-Haus, Landesgeschäftsstelle des Diakonischen Werkes, Stuttgart	134	Regional headquarters of the Diakonisches Werk religious charity, Stuttgart
138	Leybold-Werk, Alzenau bei Frankfurt am Main	138	Leybold factory, Alzenau near Frankfurt on Main
142	Landesgirokasse, Areal Reithalle, Wettbewerbsentwurf, Stuttgart	142	State Clearing Bank of Baden-Württemberg, competition design, Stuttgart
144	Landesgirokasse am Bollwerk (jetzt Landesbank Baden-Württemberg), Stuttgart	144	State Clearing Bank of Baden-Württemberg (now State Bank of Baden-Württemberg), Stuttgart
149	Landesversicherungsanstalt Schleswig-Holstein, Lübeck	149	Headquarters of State Insurance in Schleswig-Holstein, Lübeck
155	Verwaltungs- und Ausstellungsgebäude der Firma VS – Vereinigte Spezialmöbelfabriken, Tauberbischofsheim	155	Offices and exhibition space for the VS – Furniture Factory, Tauberbischofsheim
	Verkehrsbauten		**Buildings for Transport**
158	Fußgängerbereich Königstraße/Schloßplatz und U-Bahn-Station, Stuttgart	158	Pedestrian zone and underground station, Stuttgart
162	Umgestaltung des Wiener Platzes, Stuttgart-Feuerbach	162	Remodelling of Wiener Platz, Stuttgart-Feuerbach
165	Flughafenkontrollturm, Nürnberg	165	Airport control tower, Nuremberg
	Bundesbauten		**Political Buildings**
168	Bauten des Bundes und ihre Integration in die Stadt Bonn	168	New Parliament buildings, preliminary designs, Bonn
170	«Grüne Mitte», Bonn	170	"Green Centre", Bonn
171	Plenarbereich des Deutschen Bundestags, Bonn	171	Parliament building, Bonn
181	**Biographien**	181	**Biographies**
185	**Zu den vorgestellten Arbeiten**	185	**Credits for the presented buildings and projects**
191	**Werkverzeichnis**	191	**List of buildings and projects**
199	**Ausgewählte Bibliographie**	199	**Selective bibliography**
201	**Bildnachweis**	201	**Illustration credits**
203	**Über den Autor**	203	**On the author**

Einführung

Introduction

Das Werk von Behnisch & Partnern entzieht sich eindeutigen und traditionellen Klassifikationssystemen. Es gibt keinen «Behnisch-Stil», weil Behnisch und seine Mitarbeiter niemals einen solchen oder gar eine Reihe solcher produzierten. Ihre Bauten sind von meisterhafter Qualität, aber verwirrender Vielfalt; sie wechseln von einem Thema zum nächsten. Auch läßt sich kein einheitlicher theoretischer Standpunkt bestimmen, denn anstatt nur eine einzige Strategie zu verfolgen, hat das Büro ein sich immer weiter ausdehnendes Netz von Ideen vertreten. Eine zusätzliche Schwierigkeit für Historiker – und für solche, die Trost in Designer-Etiketten finden – ist die fehlende Eindeutigkeit der Urheberschaft. Das Werk trägt durchaus nicht konsequent die persönliche Handschrift von Günter Behnisch,[1] denn er sieht sich nicht gezwungen, eine solche anzuwenden, und in den meisten Fällen fertigt er die Zeichnungen nicht selber an.[2]

Jedes Büro, das mit der Planung großer Bauvorhaben befaßt ist, muß viele Leute beschäftigen, aber gewöhnlich bleiben die wichtigen Entscheidungen dem Chef oder den Partnern vorbehalten, und selbst die Zeichenmethode wird vorgeschrieben, um ein erkennbares durchgehendes Erscheinungsbild zu erzielen.[3] Behnisch und seine Partner halten die Mitarbeiter an der lockeren Leine und ermutigen sie, ihre eigenen Ideen zu produzieren und zu entwickeln, leiten sie aber beständig mit Vorschlägen und Kritik, verweisen auf Schwierigkeiten, regen Visionen an und konzentrieren sich auf brauchbare Ideen. Hunderte von jungen Architekten und Studienabsolventen sind durch das Büro gegangen; sie arbeiten im allgemeinen an einem oder zwei Projekten mit und gehen dann fort, um ihre jugendliche Energie und ihre frischen Ideen dort anzuwenden, wo sie eine Chance bekommen, etwas Eigenes unter der erforderlichen Leitung und technischen Unterstützung zu realisieren.[4] Außerdem gibt es eine lange Reihe von Partnern: Bruno Lambart von 1952 bis 1960, Fritz Auer und Carlo Weber von 1966 bis 1980, Winfried Büxel von 1966 bis 1992, Erhard Tränkner von 1966 bis 1993 und Manfred Sabatke von 1970 bis heute. Seit 1992 unterhält Behnisch ein zweites Büro, heute unter dem Namen Behnisch, Behnisch & Partner mit seinem Sohn

The work of Behnisch & Partners defies the obvious and traditional schemes of classification. There is no "Behnisch style" because Behnisch and his co-workers never produced one, nor even a series of styles. Their buildings are of masterly quality but bewildering variety, swinging from one set of concerns to another. Nor is there a unified theoretical standpoint, for rather than reflecting a single view, the office has been sustained by an evolving network of ideas. A further difficulty for historians – and for those who find consolation in designer-labels – is the lack of clarity of authorship. The work does not consistently bear the personal signature of Günter Behnisch,[1] for he feels no compulsion to impose one, and mostly he does not draw.[2]

Any office involved with sizeable buildings must employ many people, but usually the main decisions are reserved for the boss or partners and even the drawing method is dictated to produce a consistent identifiable image.[3] Behnisch and his partners allow the assistants a looser rein, encouraging them to produce and develop their own ideas, but constantly guiding them with suggestions and criticism, pointing out difficulties, reinforcing visions and concentrating the workable ideas. Hundreds of young and newly qualified architects have passed through the office, generally staying for one or two buildings before moving on, exchanging their youthful energy and fresh ideas for a chance to realise something with the necessary managerial and technical support.[4] There has also been a long series of partners: Bruno Lambart from 1952 to 1960; Fritz Auer and Carlo Weber from 1966 to 1980; Winfried Büxel from 1966 to 1992; Erhard Tränkner from 1966 to 1993; and Manfred Sabatke from 1970 to the present. Since 1992, Behnisch has also shared a second office, today known as Behnisch, Behnisch & Partner with his son Stefan, and since 1997 also with Günther Schaller. All of these people have undoubtedly made strong creative contributions, but Günter Behnisch is the central figure who made it all possible, and it is not obvious how.

The buildings are not just his. Many are managed by job architects who provide the largest share of creative ef-

Stefan und seit 1997 mit Günther Schaller. All diese Personen haben zweifellos entscheidende kreative Beiträge geleistet; Günter Behnisch ist jedoch die zentrale Figur, die alles – wie auch immer – ermöglicht hat.

Die Bauwerke stammen nicht nur von ihm. Viele wurden von Projektarchitekten ausgeführt, die den größten Anteil am kreativen Prozeß haben, aber alle sind das Ergebnis von Teamwork. Diese kann sich über einen langen Zeitraum erstrecken, denn die bevorzugte Ausführungsmethode des Büros ist die Überwachung von Baustelle und Etat in einer Hand und die Arbeit mit einem ganztägig anwesenden Bauleiter als Mitglied des Teams. Das erfordert ein ungewöhnliches Maß an Flexibilität in Entwurf und Detailplanung während der Bauzeit, wenn nicht gar Veränderungen zu einem späteren Zeitpunkt.[5] Die lange Planungsdauer bietet Zeit für Überlegungen und Verbesserungen, auch zur Improvisation. Die endgültige Ausstattung und Farbgestaltung wurden oft erst auf der Baustelle beim Erleben der Räume entschieden und Flächen manchmal durch Überstreichen geändert.

Es gibt keine Vorschrift, daß Bauten bis zum letzten Detail in Zeichnungen festgelegt werden sollen oder müssen, und aus diesem Grunde besteht auch kein Kult der Zeichnung per se: Häufig sind reale Modelle wichtiger für die Entwicklung eines Projekts. Nichts kann jedoch als adäquater Ersatz für das gebaute Ergebnis gelten, das schließlich einen Charakter ausdrückt, der über den gesamten Verlauf des Prozesses erkannt und entwickelt wurde. Mitarbeiter, die ihre ersten Bauten bei Behnisch realisierten, haben später exemplarische Bauwerke in ganz Deutschland ausgeführt. Einige Splittergruppen, darunter auch Expartner des Büros Behnisch, gehören heute zu den besten Architekten des Landes.[6] Keine andere deutsche Architektenpartnerschaft der Nachkriegszeit vermochte so konsequent hohe Qualität bei gleichzeitig derart kreativer Vielfalt über so viele Jahre durchzuhalten. Ebendiese Kombination zeichnet Günter Behnischs Büro vor allen anderen aus; sie zeugt von seiner persönlichen Begabung, gute Mitarbeiter auszuwählen, als Kritiker und Förderer von Ideen zu wirken, als Wissensquelle und als väterlicher Ratgeber zu fungieren, als Bollwerk gegen den Druck der Bürokratie und der Politik.

Günter Behnischs frühe Lebensjahre

Günter Behnisch wurde 1922 in einem Dorf bei Dresden in der Südostecke Deutschlands nahe der tschechischen Grenze geboren. Sein Vater war Lehrer, seine Mutter Hausfrau, seine Vorfahren waren Handwerker und Fuhrleute.[7] Nach einer glücklichen und beschützten frühen Kindheit kam er im Alter von zehn Jahren nach Dresden ans Gymnasium; ein Jahr später, 1933, erfolgte die Machtübernahme durch die Nationalsozialisten. Unmit-

fort, and all represent teamwork. This may take place over an extended period, for the preferred method of building has been for the office to manage site and budget, working with a full-time site architect as part of the team. It has meant an unusual degree of flexibility in design, with detail development during building, and even changes at a late stage.[5] The long design period gives time for reflection and enrichment, even for improvisation. Final finishes and colour schemes have often been determined on site with experience of the spaces, areas sometimes being readjusted by overpainting. There is no pretence that buildings can or should be predetermined down to the last detail in drawings, and for this reason there is no cult of the drawing per se: often physical models are more important for design development. But nothing is regarded as an adequate substitute for the built result, which finally defines a character discovered and developed over the whole course of the process.

Assistants who completed their first buildings with Behnisch have gone on to build exemplary work across Germany, and splinter-groups including ex-partners from the firm are now among the best practitioners in the country.[6] No other German architectural operation of the post-war period has sustained such consistent high quality over so many years and at the same time shown such creative diversity. It is this combination that makes Günter Behnisch's office unique and reveals his personal talent as selector of employees, as critic and promoter of ideas, as reservoir of wisdom, as paternal guide, as bulwark against bureaucratic and political pressures.

Günter Behnisch: the Early Life

Günter Behnisch was born in 1922 in a village near Dresden in the south-east corner of Germany close to the Czech border. His father was a school teacher, his mother a housewife, his forebears craftsmen and carters.[7] After a happy and secure childhood he went at the age of ten to study in a high-school at Dresden, but only a year later in 1933 the Nazis came to power. An immediate effect was that his father, a social democrat and opponent of the regime, lost his teaching job. Two years later he was reappointed to a school in the industrial city of Chemnitz and the family was uprooted. In 1939, when Behnisch was 17, he was called up for war service and joined the navy. He became a submariner, and by 1944 at the age of 22 had risen to the rank of submarine commander. At the end of the war he surrendered his submarine and was sent as a prisoner of war first to Scotland, then to an officer-camp in Northumberland where he remained for nearly two years. Since there were intelligent and highly-qualified people from diverse backgrounds, they set up their own classes as a kind of university within the camp. He began

telbar danach verlor sein Vater als Sozialdemokrat und Gegner des Regimes seine Arbeit, erhielt allerdings zwei Jahre später wieder eine Lehrerstelle in der Industriestadt Chemnitz, was die Familie zur völligen Neuorientierung zwang. 1939, im Alter von 17 Jahren, wurde Behnisch zur Kriegsmarine eingezogen, wo er 1944 mit 22 Jahren Kommandant eines Unterseeboots wurde. Bei Kriegsende übergab er es den Engländern und kam in Kriegsgefangenschaft, zunächst nach Schottland, dann für fast zwei Jahre in ein Offizierscamp in Northumberland. Dessen intelligente und hochqualifizierte Insassen verschiedenster Herkunft gründeten eigene Studiengänge als eine Art Universität innerhalb des Lagers. Behnisch begann dort Architektur zu studieren unter Berndt Koesters, einem ehemaligen Assistenten von Paul Schmitthenner. So wurde er in die solide und traditionelle Technik des Bauens eingeführt, für welche die «Stuttgarter Schule» bekannt geworden war. Nach seiner Entlassung 1947 kehrte Behnisch nach Deutschland zurück, hatte jedoch Bedenken, zu seinen Eltern in die Sowjetzone zu gehen. Er blieb im Westen und arbeitete in Osnabrück auf dem Bau, um praktische Erfahrungen zu sammeln, während er sich um einen Studienplatz bemühte. Er wurde an der Technischen Hochschule Stuttgart angenommen, wo er von Herbst 1947 bis zum Sommer 1951 studierte.

Die Hochschule befand sich in einem Übergangsstadium. Die Nachfolger von Paul Bonatz und Paul Schmitthenner an der von den Nationalsozialisten geförderten «Stuttgarter Schule» waren noch im Amt, während die Anhänger der Moderne sich nach zwölf Jahren Unterdrückung wieder zu etablieren versuchten.[8] Deren zentrale Figur war Richard Döcker, ehemaliger Bauleiter der berühmten Weißenhofsiedlung, der 1947 zum Professor für Städtebau berufen wurde. Zwischen beiden Gruppen kam es zu Differenzen, aber Behnisch und seine Kommilitonen waren bereit, sowohl von der einen wie von der anderen zu lernen. Sie fanden die Vertreter der Moderne – nicht nur Döcker, sondern auch Gutbrod, Gutbier und Volkart – interessanter und progressiver, jedoch aufgrund ihres langjährigen Ausschlusses auch weiter entfernt von der Praxis. Die organische Architektur Hugo Härings und Hans Scharouns wurde an der Hochschule von Heinrich Lauterbach vertreten, aber dessen Einfluß ist Behnisch eher im Hinblick auf seine Persönlichkeit und Einfühlsamkeit und nicht als gestalterisches Vorbild in Erinnerung.[9] Es gab auch wichtige Einflüsse von außerhalb und aus dem Ausland, vermittelt vor allem durch die von Alfons Leitl herausgegebene führende Zeitschrift *Baukunst und Werkform*. Die Anregungen kamen aus Amerika, aus Skandinavien und aus der benachbarten Schweiz: sowohl viele Versionen einer «regionalen Moderne» als auch der «Internationale Stil».

to study architecture under Berndt Koesters, a former assistant of Paul Schmitthenner. He was thus initiated into the solid and traditional craft construction techniques for which the "Stuttgart School" had become known. Released in 1947, he returned to Germany, but doubted the safety of joining his parents in the Soviet zone. Instead he remained in the West, working on a building site in Osnabrück to gain practical experience while he sought a place at a school of architecture. He was accepted at the Technical University in Stuttgart where he trained from the autumn of 1947 to the summer of 1951.

The school was in a transitional phase. Followers of Paul Bonatz and Paul Schmitthenner, the "Stuttgart School" favoured by the Nazis, were still present, while the Modernists struggled to re-establish themselves after 12 years of oppression.[8] The key Modernist figure was Richard Döcker, the former site architect of the famous Weissenhofsiedlung, who was made Professor for Planning and Design in 1947. There was a rift between the two groups, but Behnisch and his fellow students were prepared to learn from both. They found the Modernists – not only Döcker but Gutbrod, Gutbier, Volkart – more exciting and progressive, but out of touch with building due to long exclusion from practice. The organic direction of Hugo Häring and Hans Scharoun was represented in the school by Heinrich Lauterbach, but Behnisch remembers his influence more in terms of his personality and sensibility than as a design example.[9] There was considerable influence from outside and abroad, notably through the leading periodical *Baukunst und Werkform* edited by Alfons Leitl. Influence came from America, from Scandinavia, and from nearby Switzerland. There were many versions of "regional modernism" as well as the "international style".

The beginning of the Behnisch Office

On leaving the Technical University, Behnisch went to work for Rolf Gutbrod, an architect twelve years his senior whom he had met as teacher. Gutbrod is known mainly for the Stuttgart Liederhalle built in the mid 1950s, and also for various buildings with tent roofs designed in collaboration with Frei Otto, especially those at Mecca. He was the leading exponent in post-war Stuttgart of the organic tendency, that is of irregular architecture responsive to place and function,[10] and may have been a seminal influence in Behnisch's later concern for *Situationsarchitektur*. After a year with Gutbrod, success in an architectural competition entered with former fellow student Bruno Lambart led him and Behnisch to set up a partnership. The prize-winning school in Schwäbisch Gmünd was quickly followed by several other competition successes in the same region. The two architects

Die Anfänge des Büros Behnisch

Nach Abschluß seines Studiums an der Technischen Hochschule arbeitete Behnisch beim zwölf Jahre älteren Architekten Rolf Gutbrod, der sein Lehrer gewesen war. Gutbrod ist vor allem durch die Mitte der fünfziger Jahre errichtete Stuttgarter Liederhalle bekannt geworden, aber auch durch verschiedene Bauten mit Zeltdächern, die er in Zusammenarbeit mit Frei Otto entwickelte, besonders in Mekka. Er war der führende Vertreter des organischen Bauens im Nachkriegs-Stuttgart, das heißt einer nicht rektangulären Architektur, die auf den Ort und die Funktion reagiert,[10] und hatte vermutlich einen latenten Einfluß auf Behnischs späteres Engagement für eine «Situationsarchitektur». Nach einjähriger Tätigkeit bei Gutbrod gewannen Behnisch und sein früherer Kommilitone Bruno Lambart einen Wettbewerb und gingen eine Partnerschaft ein. Dem preisgekrönten Entwurf für eine Schule in Schwäbisch Gmünd folgten bald weitere Wettbewerbserfolge in der Region. Beide Architekten arbeiteten mit zwei Assistenten Seite an Seite in einem kleinen Büro – eine Arbeitsform, die sie auch freundschaftlich beibehielten, als sie dank weiterer Aufträge expandieren konnten. Sie nahmen erfolgreich an Wettbewerben in Nordrhein-Westfalen, der Heimat Lambarts, teil, was die Gründung eines dortigen Büros erforderlich machte. Dies wurde auch zum Anlaß für die Trennung, die 1960 in Freundschaft erfolgte. Behnisch übernahm das Stuttgarter Büro, welches bis 1966 nur seinen Namen trug.[11] Die von ihnen ausgeführten Bauten waren von hoher Qualität, aber zeittypisch und trugen noch kaum Hinweise auf das künftige progressive Werk. Im Nachhinein betrachtet, ist jedoch die Vielfalt bezeichnend, welche andeutet, daß Behnisch und Lambart sich nicht beeilten, einen durchgängigen Stil zu etablieren. Niemand würde vermuten, daß die Vogelsangschule (1961) und das Hohenstaufen-Gymnasium (1959) (S. 28 bzw. S. 26) von den gleichen Architekten stammen. Erstere ist von dem Hanggrundstück und dem Pavillongrundriß bestimmt, in freier Anordnung und konventioneller Bauweise. Das Hohenstaufen-Gymnasium in Göppingen spricht eine ganz andere Sprache: die der Standardisierung und Vorfertigung. Es repräsentiert den Beginn einer entscheidenden Periode im Büro Behnisch, die fast zehn Jahre dauerte.

Die Phase der Präfabrikation

In den fünfziger und sechziger Jahren waren die Architekten davon überzeugt, daß die Übernahme von Henry Fords Produktionssystem eine Revolution im Bauen bewirken und sich als wirtschaftlich erfolgreich erweisen würde.[12] Die Idee bestand seit den zwanziger Jahren, aber erst nach dem Zweiten Weltkrieg bot sich die Chance, sie

Rolf Gutbrod. Loba-Haus, Stuttgart, 1955
Rolf Gutbrod. Loba building, Stuttgart, 1955

worked together in a small office with two assistants drawing side by side, an arrangement which continued amicably as they gained jobs and expanded. They started to win competitions in Lambart's native Nordrhein-Westfalen, which necessitated setting up a second office there, and this prompted the practice to split. They parted on friendly terms in 1960, Behnisch taking the Stuttgart end, which remained in his name alone until 1966.[11] The buildings they had produced were of high quality but typical for their time, showing little hint of the progressive work to come. Significant with hindsight, though, is the variety, suggesting that Behnisch and Lambart were in no hurry to establish a consistent style. Nobody would guess that the Vogelsang school (1961) and Hohenstaufen school (1959) (p. 26, p. 28), were by the same architects. Vogelsang is dictated by its hillside site and pavilion plan, with free placing of elements and conventional construction. The Hohenstaufen grammar school at Göppingen tells a quite different story: that of modularisation and prefabrication. It represents the beginning of a crucial period in the Behnisch office which lasted nearly ten years.

The prefabrication phase

In the 1950s and 60s architects were convinced that the adoption of Ford's production line would cause a revolution in building and prove economically advantageous.[12] The idea had been around since the 1920s, but only after the Second World War came the chance to test it at a large scale. There was an extensive building programme

in großem Maßstab zu testen. Es gab ein umfangreiches Wiederaufbauprogramm, aber nur wenig ausgebildete Handwerker, und die neuen Technologien waren besser geeignet für die Bedingungen in der Fabrik als für den Schlamm der Baustelle. Die frühen Modernen hatten die Stadtzentren als düster und ungesund erkannt, und die Transportmöglichkeiten hatten sich verbessert. Deshalb wurden wegen der Sonne und Luft Grundstücke am Stadtrand gewählt, die der Gesundheit zuträglicher waren, und die Neubauten waren freistehende Objekte in der Landschaft. Die saubere, klare, ordentliche und monotone, als «Internationaler Stil» bezeichnete Architektur schien für das moderne Leben angemessen: Ihre Effizienz mußte nur bewiesen werden, indem man sie auf geeignete Weise mit der Massenproduktion verband.

Zuerst kam die Standardisierung, dann die Vorfabrikation. Die Fachhochschule Ulm von 1963 (S. 30) sieht dem früheren Hohenstaufen-Gymnasium ähnlich, da beide horizontale Gebäude mit strengem Rhythmus und einheitlichen Elementen sind. Bei näherem Hinschauen zeigen sich jedoch grundlegende Unterschiede. Göppingen verwendet ein umfassenderes Vokabular und viel Ortbeton, während Ulm ganz aus vorgefertigten Elementen hergestellt wurde, was eine strengere Disziplin erforderte. In Göppingen wechselt der konstruktive Rhythmus mit den Geschossen, und die Treppenschächte sind extra breit, während Ulm sich strikt an das 3 m-Modul hält.

Zu Beginn der sechziger Jahre arbeitete das Büro Behnisch mit der Firma Rostan in Friedrichshafen zusammen und produzierte ein vorgefertigtes Betonsystem nach der holländischen Schockbeton-Methode; die Ulmer Hochschule stellte den Prototyp dar. Die Elemente wurden so groß wie möglich gemacht und auf vibrierenden Platten gegossen, um die Form genau einzuhalten. Danach transportierte man sie mit Lastwagen zur Baustelle, wo sie mit Hilfe eines Krans montiert wurden. Der unmittelbare Vorteil lag in der Schnelligkeit der Montage; die Methode versprach jedoch, unendlich wiederholbar zu sein. Behnisch und sein Team faszinierten zwei widersprüchliche Herausforderungen: die Notwendigkeit, ein System zu entwerfen, das allen Bedingungen gerecht wird, und die maximalen Variationsmöglichkeiten, um endlose Wiederholungen zu vermeiden. Dieser Gegensätzlichkeit ließ sich auf zwei Ebenen Rechnung tragen: Das System konnte mit Wänden oder Stützen in vielfachen Kombinationen und für hohe oder niedrige, lange oder kurze, monolithische oder in Pavillons aufgelöste Schulbauten verwendet werden.[13]

Nach dem Erfolg des Ulmer Gebäudes wurden Behnisch und sein Team aufgefordert, ein weitere Fachhochschule in Aalen zu errichten – ihr erster staatlicher Auftrag ohne Wettbewerb. Mit der Absicht zu beweisen, daß der repe-

but a lack of trained craftsmen, and new technologies were better suited to factory conditions than to the mud of the building site. Early modernists had come to regard city centres as dark and unhealthy, and transport had improved, so peripheral sites were chosen for sunlight and air which would guarantee good health, and new buildings became free-standing objects in the landscape. The clean, straight, orderly and repetitive architecture dubbed "International Style" seemed appropriate to modern life: its efficiency needed only to be proven by tying it properly to mass-production.

First came standardisation, then prefabrication. The engineering school at Ulm of 1963 (p. 30) seems similar to the earlier Hohenstaufen grammar school at Göppingen, both being linear buildings with a strong rhythm and repeated components, but a closer look reveals fundamental differences. Göppingen uses a wider range of building vocabularies and much in-situ concrete, while Ulm was built entirely of prefabricated components, demanding a tighter discipline. At Göppingen the structural rhythm changes between floors, and stair bays are extra-wide, while Ulm follows the 3 m module strictly.

In the early 1960s the Behnisch office collaborated with the firm Rostan of Friedrichshafen to produce a precast concrete system using the Dutch Schock-Beton method, and the Ulm building was the prototype. The units were made as large as possible and cast on vibrating tables to assure accurate shaping. They were transported to site on lorries and assembled by crane. The immediate advantage was speed of assembly, but the promise of the method

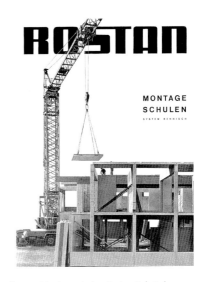

Firma Rostan, Montageschulen, System Behnisch, Friedrichshafen, 1963
Rostan Company, prefabrication system for schools, Behnisch system, Friedrichshafen, 1963

titive Charakter des Systems durch phantasievolle Planung überwunden werden könnte, verwendeten sie es Mitte der sechziger Jahre weiterhin bei mehreren Schulen (S. 33), verloren jedoch allmählich den Mut. Die vorgefertigten Systeme waren schnell, erzielten aber nie die versprochene Wirtschaftlichkeit, und wenn sie einmal entwickelt waren, wurden sie von den Bauämtern und großen Baufirmen phantasielos angewendet. So führten sie schließlich nicht zu einer Verbesserung der Architektur, sondern dienten als verkürztes Verfahren dazu, eine solche zu verhindern. Im Rückblick auf diese Phase bemerkte Behnisch 1987:

«Später waren uns die bei diesen Entwicklungen entstandenen engen geometrischen Ordnungen lästig... Heute meinen wir, daß solche ‹Ordnungen› Instrumente zum Zwecke der Herrschaft sein können, um Planungsvorgänge, darüber hinaus Architektur und letztlich Leben beherrschen zu können, wenn deren Lebendigkeit und Vielfältigkeit eher als bedrohlich empfunden wird... Aber schon damals leuchtete die Gefahr auf, die dann später in Universitätsbauten und Großkliniken Realität wurde; zumindest konnte geahnt werden, daß dann, wenn der durch Techniken scheinbar vorgezeigte Weg konsequent gegangen würde, Architektur tendenziell einseitig werden müßte und nicht mehr Wünschen und Bedürfnissen unterschiedlichster Art entsprechen könnte und auch nicht mehr die mögliche Vielfalt unserer Welt einfangen und widerspiegeln könnte.»[14]

Ende der sechziger Jahre gab Behnisch die gerasterten Grundrisse und sich wiederholenden Elemente auf und verwendete ein breiteres und vielfältigeres Vokabular. Anstatt sich nach den konstruktiven Erfordernissen zu richten, ging er mehr auf den Ort und das soziale Umfeld ein. Das Büro wurde auch größer. Schon Mitte der sechziger Jahre beschäftigte es etwa ein Dutzend Architekten, und in Anbetracht seiner zunehmend wichtigeren Aufgaben gründete Behnisch 1966 eine Partnerschaft mit Auer, Büxel, Tränkner und Weber; 1970 kam Sabatke als weiterer Partner hinzu. Sie arbeiteten dann an ihrem größten und bedeutendsten Auftrag.

Der Münchener Olympiapark

Der 1967 geplante Olympiapark diente den Spielen von 1972. Die späten sechziger Jahre waren eine Zeit des sozialen Umbruchs und der Befreiung, des politischen Idealismus. 1968 fanden die Studentenrevolten statt, die Anti-Vietnam-Demonstrationen und sogar hinter dem Eisernen Vorhang der tragischerweise kurzlebige Prager Frühling. Die Jugendkultur gab sich eine neue Identität, und die alten sozialen Hierarchien wurden in Frage gestellt. Spontaneität und Zwanglosigkeit wurden gepriesen, Gleichheit und Brüderlichkeit proklamiert, während

Olympiapark, München, 1972. Luftbild des zentralen Bereichs
Olympic Park, Munich, 1972. Aerial view of central area

was that it could be endlessly reapplied. Behnisch and his team were attracted by two opposed challenges: the need to design a system dealing with all conditions, and the provision of maximal variation to prevent excessive repetition. This variety could be achieved at two levels: the system could operate with walls or columns in various combinations, and schools could be designed tall or flat, long or short, monolithic or subdivided into pavilions.[13]

Following the success of the building at Ulm, Behnisch and his team were asked to build another at Aalen – their first commission from the state without competition. Intent on proving that the repetitive nature of the system could be overcome by imaginative design, they went on in the mid 1960s to use the system in a series of schools (p. 33), but gradually they lost heart. Prefabricated systems were quick, but the promised economies were never achieved, and once they had been developed, they were used unimaginatively by local authorities and large building firms. They ended up less a way of improving architecture than as a short-cut for avoiding it altogether. Reconsidering this phase in 1987, Behnisch remarked that:

"The geometric discipline became oppressive... Such 'ordering systems' can become instruments of domination, first taking over design processes, then moving on to architecture and finally to life itself, whose vitality and variety comes to be regarded by the system-minded as a threat... The danger which later became a reality in new university buildings and massive hospitals was already beginning to show itself. We could see that if architecture followed this purely technical direction, it would necessarily become one-sided, unable to express wishes and requirements of a differentiated kind, unable to respond to and reflect the possible variety of our world."[14]

From the late 1960s onwards, Behnisch work moved away from gridded plans and repeated elements, adopt-

Fahnen und Uniformen als Symbole der alten Ordnung verworfen oder parodiert wurden. Das Münchener Olympiagelände war ein Treffpunkt für gleichberechtigte Bürger aus aller Welt. Mehr als jede andere Nachkriegsanlage sollte es das demokratische Gesicht der neuen Bundesrepublik ausdrücken. Die letzte Olympiade in Deutschland hatte 1936 in Berlin stattgefunden und war von Hitler dazu benutzt worden, die Macht des «Dritten Reiches» und die Überlegenheit der «arischen Rasse» zu demonstrieren. Werner Marchs Bauten waren axial und imperialistisch, geplant, um durch ihren gewaltigen Maßstab zu beeindrucken und einzuschüchtern, und vervollständigt durch Skulpturen heroischer Figuren zur Glorifizierung des Siegerkultes.[15]

Die Münchener Olympiade war von all diesem weit entfernt. Statt axialer Formalität als Abbild der Unterwerfung des Volkes unter den Willen *eines* Mannes war eine eher informelle Wirkung vonnöten sowie die Betonung der Gleichberechtigung aller Teilnehmer. Große Menschenansammlungen weckten bedrückende Erinnerungen; Massenhysterie mußte vermieden werden. Anderen Ländern sollte ein liberales und menschliches Deutschland vorgeführt werden, in dem man gleichberechtigt wetteiferte. Das große Gelände im Norden Münchens wurde gewählt, um eine «Olympiade im Grünen» zu ermöglichen, und war von Anfang an als bleibendes Erholungsgebiet für die Stadt vorgesehen.

Obgleich der Münchener Olympiapark vor allem durch seine Silhouette – die berühmten Seilnetzdächer – bekannt wurde, beruht die Planung ebenso auf der genialen Gestaltung des Geländes, wodurch die gewaltigen Tribünen der Stadien, alle Versorgungsbereiche und vieles andere unter einer grünen Decke verschwinden (S. 65).[16] Dies hat offensichtlich Auswirkungen auf spätere, in den Boden gesetzte Bauten gehabt, zum Beispiel die vielen abgesenkten Sporthallen (S. 76, 78, 82), die unterirdischen Magazine der Bibliothek in Eichstätt (S. 110) oder den tiefer gelegten Innenhof des Bildungszentrums in Stuttgart-Birkach (S. 44). In der Tat spielen die meisten nachfolgenden Bauten von Behnisch in irgendeiner Weise mit dem Gelände und kontrastieren in der Behandlung der Elemente über und unter der Erde. Aber nicht nur die neue Einstellung zur Landschaft und zur Form veränderte nach dem Olympia-Auftrag das Büro Behnisch.[17] Als Symbol der Aufgeschlossenheit Westdeutschlands auf dem Höhepunkt des Wirtschaftswunders stellte der Staat Geld in einer heute kaum mehr vorstellbaren Menge zur Verfügung. Der ehrgeizige Wettbewerbsentwurf war in mancher Hinsicht wenig mehr als eine Skizze. Um ihn weiterzuentwickeln und zu realisieren, mußte Behnisch seine Mitarbeiterzahl um ein Vielfaches vergrößern und ein Büro in München eröffnen, da die Ausführungspla-

ing a broader and more varied vocabulary. Instead of taking a cue from constructional requirements, it became more responsive to place and social content. The office was also growing. Even in the mid 1960s it already employed around a dozen architects, and in recognition of their increasingly important role Behnisch formed a partnership in 1967 with Auer, Büxel, Tränkner and Weber; Sabatke joined as a further partner in 1970. They were working on their largest and most prestigious commission.

The Munich Olympic Park

The Olympic Park, conceived in 1967, was used for the games of 1972. The late 1960s was a time of social change and liberation, of political idealism. 1968 saw student revolutions, anti-Vietnam rallies, and even behind the iron curtain the tragically short-lived Prague Spring. Youth-culture found a new identity, and old social hierarchies were thrown into question. Spontaneity and informality were celebrated, equality and fraternity proclaimed, while flags and uniforms as signs of the old order were rejected or parodied. The Munich Olympic site was a meeting place on equal terms for citizens of the world. More than any other building since the war, it was required to show the democratic face of the new Federal Republic. The previous German Olympics had been held in Berlin in 1936, used by Hitler to show the power of the Third Reich and superiority of the Aryan Race. Werner March's buildings were axial and imperialistic, designed to impress and intimidate with their huge scale, and complemented by sculptures of heroic figures glorifying the cult of the victor.[15] The Munich Olympics reversed all this. Instead of axial formality reflecting the subordination of a nation to one man's will, a sense of informality was needed, and a stress on the equality of participants. Large gatherings evoked nervous memories, and mass-hysteria was to be avoided. Other countries were to be shown a liberal and humane Germany competing on equal terms. The large site to the north of Munich was chosen to allow "Olympics in a green setting", and was conceived from the start as a permanent recreational park for the city.

Though best known for its skyscapes – the famous cable-net roofs – the design of the Olympic Park depends equally on the ingenious groundscapes which swallow the huge banks of arena seating, all the servicing provision, and much else under a green blanket (p. 65).[16] This has obvious implications for later buildings set into the ground, like the many sunken sports halls (p. 76, 78, 82), the sunken bookstore of the Eichstätt library (p. 110), or the sunken court at the Birkach seminary (p. 44). In fact most later Behnisch buildings play with the groundplane in some way, contrasting the treatment of things above

nung ausschließlich dort erfolgte, und er arbeitete eng mit Ingenieuren, Sonderfachleuten und anderen Firmen zusammen.[18] Die vielen beteiligten Interessenvertreter und einflußreichen Persönlichkeiten hätten erdrückend wirken und zu Verwässerung oder Kompromissen führen können, aber Behnisch behielt die Führung in der Hand und brachte alle dazu, an einem Strang zu ziehen. Die Erfahrung erwies den Wert seines Agierens als Kritiker und Manager anstatt als eigentlicher Planer – einer Methode, die, wenn erfolgreich angewendet, zu einem größeren Spielraum an Kreativität führt. Vielen Architekten gelingt es nicht, diesen Übergang zu meistern, sie finden ihren Weg nicht, und ihre Bauten werden langweilig, wirken bürokratisch. Der Schlüssel zu Behnischs Erfolg ist seine Begabung, die Kreativität anderer nutzbar zu machen und zu lenken. Es bedarf der Aufgeschlossenheit und eines phantasievollen Scharfblicks, um zu erkennen, in welche Richtung eine Idee sich entwickeln kann. Es setzt auch voraus, daß Architektur Teamwork ist, zu dem viele beitragen können.

Situationsarchitektur

Der Erfolg von München führte nicht gleich zu neuen Aufträgen, erweiterte jedoch das Potential des Büros und bewirkte neues Selbstvertrauen sowie eine Bereitschaft zur Innovation. Nach wie vor gingen Aufträge vorwiegend aufgrund von Wettbewerben ein, in denen die Architekten in den siebziger und achtziger Jahren fortlaufend Preise gewannen, vor allem für Sozialbauten wie Schulen, Kindergärten und Altenheime. Die Entwicklung während dieser Periode ist eine Geschichte der wachsenden Freiheit und Verbesserung der Konzeption, aber auch der kritischen Auseinandersetzung mit dem Gleichgewicht zwischen den Teilen und dem Ganzen. Allgemein läßt sich feststellen, daß das Vokabular sich erweitert, freier und mutiger wird und man sich in zunehmendem Maße mit den spezifischen Aspekten jedes Projektes befaßt – mit der jeweiligen Situation. Das Gelände und die Umgebung sind immer von Bedeutung, und jeder Bau wird als eine Zusammensetzung von Räumen oder Volumen aufgefaßt und nicht als finites Objekt oder ein Ding an sich. In einer Ansprache Mitte der achtziger Jahre formulierte Behnisch dies wie folgt:
«Das Ziel der Architektenarbeit ist nicht das Haus, das Gebäude, vielmehr die zu schaffende Situation. Und nur solche Maßnahmen sind zu treffen, die die – im Glücksfall ohnehin schon vorhandene – Situation verdeutlichen, verstärken, erhöhen, oder in weniger glücklichen Fällen: neu schaffen. Was bedeutet, daß Einzelheiten von der speziellen Situation her entschieden und bestimmt werden, daß eigentlich immer neue spezielle Fassungen gefragt sind.»[19]

with things below. But the new attitude to landscape and form was only part of the way in which the Olympic job changed the Behnisch office.[17] As a symbol of West German sophistication at the height of an economic boom, the state poured money into it in a way scarcely imaginable today. The ambitious competition design was in some ways little more than a sketch. To develop and execute it, Behnisch largely extended his staff, opening a branch in Munich to supervise execution, and worked closely with other firms.[18] The many interests and powerful personalities involved could have been overwhelming, leading to dilution or compromise, but Behnisch guided it through, persuading all to pull together. The experience proved the worth of acting as critic and manager rather than making designs directly, a method which, if successful, allows greater creative range. Many architects fail to manage this transition and lose their way, the work becoming dull and bureaucratic. The key to Behnisch's success is his gift to harness and focus the creativity of others. It requires open-mindedness and imaginative insight to see where an idea might go. It also presumes that architecture is team-work to which many may contribute.

Situationsarchitektur

The success at Munich did not immediately bring further commissions but enlarged the firm's potential, producing a fresh confidence and a readiness to innovate. The office continued to gain its work largely through competitions, winning them in a continuous stream throughout the 1970s and 80s, mainly for social buildings such as schools, kindergartens and old people's homes. The development during this period is a story of increasing freedom and sophistication of concept, but also of acute concern for the balance of part and whole. In general one can note that the vocabulary broadens, becomes freer and more daring, and there is increasing concern with the specific aspects of each project – with each *situation*. The site and surroundings are always important, and each building is understood as a society of rooms or volumes rather than a finite object or a thing in itself. Speaking in the mid 1980s, Behnisch put it as follows:

"The goal of architectural work is not just the building, but much more the situation to be created. And only such measures should be considered as somehow interpret, strengthen, or intensify the situation, whether – as in fortunate cases – it is already mainly given, or whether – in less fortunate ones – it has to be created. This means that the particularities of the special situation should play a decisive role and that new and special solutions must always be sought."[19]

Die Entwicklung verlief langsam. Die Turnhalle in Rothenburg von 1970 (S. 63) ist noch vollkommen orthogonal mit regelmäßigem Rhythmus der architektonischen Ordnung und einer fast symmetrischen Hauptfassade. Die Elemente sind aus Stahl und Glas, die Geometrie des Gebäudes ist aber noch, wie bei den vorfabrizierten Schulen, vom Montageprozeß bestimmt. Die Baumasse wird jedoch durch Absenken in den Boden reduziert, und der sichtbare Teil präsentiert sich als eleganter und schlichter Pavillon. Die das Dach tragenden Balken führen durch die Glaswand und betonen die immaterielle Wirkung der Glashaut. Hier zeigt sich schon in einfacher Form jene räumliche Durchdringung, die im späteren Werk zur Routine wird. Sie verweist auch auf den Einfluß eines ganz Großen der vorigen Generation: des holländischen Architekten Johannes Duiker.[20]

Ein weiteres Schlüsselbauwerk, das die Entwicklung des Büros in anderer Richtung kennzeichnet, ist die Schule «In den Berglen» bei Oppelsbohm von 1969 (S. 34). Obgleich der Grundriß und die Fassaden modular mit wiederholbaren Elementen geplant wurden, ist die Form polygonal mit nach außen gelegten Klassenräumen und einer zentralen Halle. Das bedeutet eine entschiedene Abkehr von der Neutralität des Rasters, denn die Gestalt ist ein geschlossenes Ganzes und kein neutraler Systembau, zwischen Zentrum und Peripherie wird deutlich unterschieden. Die Idee wurde weiterentwickelt beim Progymnasium Lorch von 1973 (S. 36), das durch asymmetrische Trakte ergänzt wurde, jedoch den Kreis als zentralen Mittelpunkt beibehielt. Von diesem Zeitpunkt an wurde der kreisförmige oder polygonale Grundriß zu einem wichtigen Planungselement, das entweder zur Bildung lokaler Zentren benutzt wurde, wie beim Postmuseum (S. 114) und dem Entwurf für die Deutsche Biblio-

Progymnasium und Realschule, Lorch/Württemberg, 1973
Grammar school, Lorch/Württemberg, 1973

It was a gradual development. The sports-hall at Rothenburg of 1970 (p. 63) is still fully orthogonal with a regular bay-rhythm and an almost symmetrical main facade. The kit of parts is steel and glass, but the geometry of the building is still conditioned by the assembly process, as with the prefabricated schools. The building's bulk is reduced by sinking it into the ground, however, the visible part being presented as an elegant and minimal pavilion. The steel beams supporting the roof pass through the glass wall, stressing the insubstantial nature of the glass skin. This shows in simple form the spatial interpenetration that was to become routine in later work. It also suggests the influence of a hero from the previous generation: the Dutch architect Johannes Duiker.[20]

Another key work significant for the firm's development in a different way is the school "In den Berglen" near Oppelsbohm of 1969 (p. 34). Although plan and facades are modular with repeated components, the figure is polygonal with perimeter classrooms and a central hall. This marks a dramatic departure from the neutrality of the grid, for the figure is a closed whole rather than an open ended system, differentiating strongly between centre and periphery. The idea was taken further in the grammar school of Lorch of 1973 (p. 36) which grew irregular wings in addition, but retained the circle as overall focus. The circular or polygonal plan-figure became from this time on an important planning element, whether used to produce local foci in a plan such as the Post Museum (p. 114) or National Library project (p. 104), or at larger scale to unify a complex as with the great ring at the Öhringen school (p. 54). It achieved social and political resonance with the parliamentary chamber at Bonn (p. 171), where MPs sit in a ring in confimation of their equal status in democracy, like monks in a medieval chapter house or the fabled Knights of the Round Table.

The circular principle is also present in less obvious forms, as with the central sunken garden at the Birkach seminary (p. 44), which is the social focus of the whole insti-

Johannes Duiker, Sanatorium Zonnestraal, Hilversum, 1928
Johannes Duiker, Zonnestraal sanatorium, Hilversum, 1928

Hans Scharoun, Philharmonie, Berlin, 1963
Hans Scharoun, Philharmonic Hall, Berlin, 1963

thek (S. 104), oder in größerem Maßstab, um einen Komplex zusammenzufassen, wie beim großen Ring der Schule in Öhringen (S. 54). Gesellschaftliche und politische Bedeutung übernahm er beim Plenarsaal in Bonn (S. 171), wo die Parlamentarier im Kreis gesetzt sind, um ihren gleichberechtigten Status in der Demokratie auszudrücken – wie Mönche in einem mittelalterlichen Domkapitel oder die legendären Ritter von König Artus' Tafelrunde.

Das Kreisprinzip ist auch in weniger eindeutigen Formen erkennbar, zum Beispiel im zentralen, tiefergelegten Garten des Bildungszentrums in Stuttgart-Birkach (S. 44), der den sozialen Mittelpunkt der ganzen Einrichtung und eine Art Kreuzgang bildet. Dieses große Projekt vom Ende der siebziger Jahre durchlief verschiedene Stadien, bis die endgültige Form festgelegt wurde, und die frühen Pläne wirken fast schematisch im Vergleich mit dem ausgeführten Bau. Zwei Arten der Verfeinerung fanden statt: erstens eine Differenzierung der Teile, um ihnen unterschiedlichen und kontrastierenden Charakter zu verleihen, und zweitens die Entdeckung der wirksamsten und geeignetsten Beziehung zwischen ihnen. Behnisch beschrieb dies wie folgt:

«Die einzelnen Bereiche ‹trieben› fast von sich aus an den passenden Platz im Gelände und im Gebäude, an ‹ihren› Ort, damit ein sinnvolles Gesamtgefüge bildend, bestimmt durch eine ungezwungene, vom Wesen des Ganzen und des Einzelnen bestimmte Ordnung, eine Ordnung, die ‹inwendig› ist.»[21]

Die organische Tradition

Hier besteht ein eindeutiger Bezug zur «organischen» Architekturtheorie Hugo Härings, der behauptete, daß Formen nicht «auferlegt», sondern «entdeckt» werden sollten, da sie im Wesen der Aufgabe liegen, der zu dienen sie bestimmt sind.[22] Härings Theorie wurde in der deutschen Nachkriegsarchitektur am erkennbarsten von Hans Scharoun übernommen, dessen Philharmonie in Berlin 1963 fertiggestellt wurde. Scharouns Grundrisse – typisch dafür seine Schulen – waren stark aufgegliedert, um einzelnen Elementen, zum Beispiel Klassenräumen, Freiheit und Individualität zu gewähren, und er verwendete komplexe, nicht-rektanguläre Geometrien, wo andere sich an das

tution and a kind of cloister. This large project, dating from the late 1970s, went through several stages before the final arrangement was defined, and the first plans seem almost schematic in comparison with the final ones. Two kinds of refinement were taking place: first a differentiation of parts to give them distinct and contrasting characters, second the discovery of the most efficient and appropriate relationship between them. Behnisch described it as follows:

"The single areas almost floated by themselves towards the appropriate positions on the site and in the building, to 'their' place, thus forming a whole that makes sense, dominated by an order that is not forced, is a part of the whole and the individual, that is 'internalised'."[21]

The Organic Tradition

There is a distinct echo here of the "organic" design philosophy of Hugo Häring, who proclaimed that forms should not be "imposed" but are waiting to be "discovered", implied in the nature of the task that they are born to serve.[22] Häring's philosophy was most clearly exemplified in post-war German architecture by Hans Scharoun, whose Berlin Philharmonie concert hall had been completed in 1963. Scharoun's plans – typically his schools – were highly articulated to give individual elements such as classrooms their freedom and individuality, and he employed complex non-rectangular geometries when others clung to the grid. He explicitly connected the formal freedom of individual parts in architecture with the idea of freedom for individuals within a democracy: an equation much reiterated by Behnisch.

During the period of systematic prefabrication, Scharoun represented the radical alternative, showing how buildings might be shaped not by technique but by the nature of the place and the activity to be housed.[23] More than any other leading German architect of his generation, Behnisch could be said to have inherited and extended the "organic" direction of Häring and Scharoun, not only in

Raster klammerten. Explizit verband er die formale Freiheit der individuellen Teile in der Architektur mit der Idee der Freiheit des Individuums in einer Demokratie: eine Gleichung, die häufig von Behnisch zitiert wurde.

Im Zeitalter der systematisierten Vorfabrikation vertrat Scharoun die radikale Alternative und zeigte, wie man Bauten nicht entsprechend der Technik, sondern dem Wesen des Ortes und der darin stattfindenden Aktivitäten zu gestalten vermag.[23] Man kann durchaus sagen, daß Behnisch mehr als jeder andere führende Architekt seiner Generation von der «organischen» Richtung Härings und Scharouns übernommen und weiterentwickelt hat, nicht nur in der Betonung der sozialen Aspekte, der geometrischen Ungebundenheit und der räumlichen Durchdringung seiner Bauwerke, sondern auch im Hinblick auf seinen theoretischen Ansatz. Bauten gehören zum Leben, sie werden zum Bestandteil eines Ortes und Schauplatz menschlicher Aktivitäten. Sie sollten nicht allzu festgelegt oder perfekt sein, und ganz gewiß sollten sie nicht primär als technische oder plastische Objekte betrachtet werden.

Der Raum gewinnt Substanz

Das Erbe ist eindeutig, aber Behnisch & Partner haben Scharoun in vielerlei Hinsicht übertroffen. Die großen Unterschiede liegen im Material. Scharoun, der erst gegen Ende seines Lebens die Chance erhielt, größere Projekte zu realisieren, konzipierte seine Entwürfe vorwiegend nach räumlichen Aspekten und behandelte die Frage der Konstruktion als sekundäres Kriterium. Behnisch und seine Mitarbeiter stiegen jedoch während ihrer Systembauperiode tief in die technische Disziplin der Tragwerke ein und verloren die konstruktive Logik nie aus dem Auge, selbst wenn sie sich dagegen entschieden und ihr eine beherrschende Rolle verweigerten. Bei Projekten wie der Hauptschule auf dem Schäfersfeld in Lorch (S. 48) und der Bibliothek in Eichstätt (S. 110) gewannen die Grundrisse nach Scharounschem Vorbild eine neue Form der materiellen Identität, und zwar dank der Überschneidung und Durchdringung der konstruktiven Schichten. Anstatt nur nach räumlichen Aspekten konzipiert zu werden, wurden sie anhand von Modellen entwickelt, und die Durchdringung der Elemente wurde auf neue Weise verstärkt. Die gleiche Technik der Schichtung ließ sich auch auf Pläne orthodoxeren Charakters anwenden, zum Beispiel beim Glasdach des Bonner Plenarsaals (S. 171), um eindrucksvolle Raumwirkungen zu erzielen, wie sie bisher noch nie erdacht oder gar erlebt worden waren.

Die aus dunklem blaugrauen Stahl und aus Glas bestehende Eingangshalle des Bonner Parlamentsgebäudes sowie gewisse Merkmale der Ansichten am Rheinufer verweisen weniger auf Scharoun als auf Mies van der Rohe oder seinen ideologischen Nachfolger im Nach-

the social articulation, geometric irregularity and interpenetrating spaces of the work, but also in terms of his philosophical approach. Buildings belong to life, they become part of a place and the site of human activities. They should not be too finite or too perfect, and certainly should not be seen primarily as technical or sculptural objects.

Giving substance to space

The inheritance is clear, but in many ways Behnisch & Partners have gone far beyond Scharoun. The big difference lies in the material side. With little chance to build until late in his career, Scharoun conceived his designs largely in spatial terms, treating the question of construction as a secondary issue. But Behnisch and his co-workers, steeped in the technical disciplines of construction during their systematic period, never lost sight of constructive logic even if they reacted against it and refused it a dominant role. In projects such as the second school at Lorch (p. 48) and the Eichstätt library (p. 110), somewhat Scharounian plans gained a new kind of material identity through the overlapping and intersecting layers of construction. Rather than being conceived in purely spatial terms, they were developed through models, and the interpenetration of elements was dramatised in a new way. The same techniques of layering could also be applied to plans of more orthodox character, as with the glazed roof of the Bonn Parliament (p. 171), to produce impressive spatial effects never seen or even thought of before.

The entrance hall to the Parliament with its dark, greyish blue steel and glass and certain of its riverside elevations

Plenarbereich des Deutschen Bundestages, Bonn, 1992.
Dahinter: Ehemaliges Abgeordnetenhochhaus «Langer Eugen», Architekt: Egon Eiermann, 1969
Parlimentary Chamber of the German Bundestag, Bonn, 1992.
In the background: former high-rise for members of parliament "Langer Eugen", architect: Egon Eiermann, 1969

kriegsdeutschland, auf Egon Eiermann. Behnisch schätzt den heute weitgehend vergessenen Eiermann hoch und ist sicherlich von dessen Fassadengliederung beeinflußt worden. Eine oberflächliche Ähnlichkeit des Parlamentsgebäudes mit Eiermanns «Langem Eugen» in Bonn ist gegebenenfalls «situationsbedingt», weil dieser direkt neben dem Plenarsaal steht. Aber bei näherer Prüfung verflüchtigt sich diese Ähnlichkeit. Behnischs Bauwerk bezieht seinen besonderen Charakter aus der Reaktion auf die asymmetrische, durch den Fluß und die bestehende Bebauung gegebene Situation. Es ist, im Gegensatz zu Eiermanns Bau, reich an beabsichtigten Unvollkommenheiten und komplexen Wechselwirkungen: Sogar auf eine große Stütze in der Eingangshalle wurde verzichtet, um die Vorherrschaft des Weges und des Raumes über das Ideal der konstruktiven Ordnung darzustellen. In Behnischs späteren Bauten ist es immer wieder die lange gesuchte und mühsam gefundene Geste als Reaktion auf den besonderen Kontext, die den speziellen Charakter erzeugt, etwa der geneigte Halbzylinder aus Glas, der im Postmuseum das Untergeschoß belichtet (S. 114), oder die große diagonale Glasscheibe, die das Foyer der Landesbank (S. 144) überdeckt. Im ersten Gebäude für das Diakonische Werk bricht und steigt eine Folge besonderer asymmetrischer Gesten aus einem Basisblock, der durch einen Bebauungsplan vorgegeben war, welcher sogar das Stützenraster festlegte (S. 134). Das Ergebnis dessen ist, daß Behnischs Gebäude wie ein leuchtendes Fanal der Individualität und des menschlichen Maßstabs aus der Menge anonymer Glaskisten herausragt.

Seit Ende der achtziger Jahre sind die Bauten aus dem Büro Behnisch zunehmend spielerischer geworden. «Das Formale ist frei», erklärte der Meister[24] und ließ Experimente in vielen Richtungen durchführen, vom formalen Extrem des Hysolar-Instituts mit seinen silbernen Containern und dem funktionslosen, aber richtungweisenden roten Holm (S. 106) bis zum bewußt schiffsähnlichen Erscheinungsbild des Kindergartens in Stuttgart-Luginsland (S. 90). Auch wurde immer mehr Farbe angewendet, darüber theoretisiert und das Verfahren verfeinert: Hier bewährte sich vor allem das Talent von Christian Kandzia,[25] aber es wurden auch spezielle Künstler beauftragt.[26] Der folgende Kommentar von Behnisch zeigt, wie ernst die Farbe zu nehmen ist, nicht als oberflächliche Dekoration, sondern als ein Symptom für weit tiefer liegende Phänomene:

«Durch Färben versuche ich, die vorgegebene Welt zu überwinden. Dabei geht es nicht nur um die Welt der Erscheinungen. Oft möchte ich eine Welt überwinden, die von Kräften dominiert wird, zum Beispiel von Kräften der Produktions-, Vertriebs-, Verwaltungsapparate. Diese drängen mich dazu, Produkte zu verwenden, die billig,

seem less like Scharoun's work than that of Mies or his ideological follower in post-war Germany Egon Eiermann. Behnisch values highly the now rather neglected Eiermann, and has certainly been influenced by his layering of facades. A superficial resemblance to Eiermann's work at Bonn is appropriately "situational" because Eiermann's Lange Eugen office block stands directly adjacent. But on closer examination the resemblance is fleeting. It is the response to the asymmetrical *situation* created by the river and existing buildings that gives Behnisch's building its special character. Unlike Eiermann's work, it is full of deliberate imperfections and complex interactions: even a main column of the entrance hall was omitted, showing the dominance of route and space over the ideal of structural order. Time and again in the later buildings, it is the long sought and hard-won gesture in response to the particular context that produces special character, like the tilted half-cylinder of glass bringing light to the basement of the Post Museum (p. 114), or the great diagonal glass plane covering the foyer of the Landesgirokasse (p. 144). In the first Diakonie offices, a battery of special irregular gestures erode and erupt from a basic block given by a master-plan which even determined the column grid (p. 134). As a result, the Behnisch building stands out as a beacon of individuality and human scale in a rank of anonymous glass boxes.

In the late 1980s and 1990s the work of the Behnisch office became increasingly playful. "All forms are possible" proclaimed the master,[24] and experiments were made in many directions, from the formal extreme of the Hysolar Institute with its silver containers and functionless but di-

Museum für Post und Kommunikation, Frankfurt am Main, 1990
Post and Communications Museum, Frankfurt on Main, 1990

Hysolar-Institutsgebäude der Universität Stuttgart, 1987
Hysolar Institute of Stuttgart University, 1987

gut zu gebrauchen und vielleicht haltbar sind. Aber sie gefallen mir nicht. Damit möchte ich mich nicht gemein machen. Und ich möchte die Gegenstände dieser Welt sichtbar nicht um mich haben. Als unsichtbare Gehilfen sind sie mir willkommen, als Gehilfen, die dort, wo sie dann sichtbar ins Bild meiner Welt treten, schöne Kleider tragen müssen – wie in alten Zeiten am Hofe. ... Man sollte sich intensiv beschäftigen mit dem Farblichen. Das kostet nicht viel, ist frei und wirkungsvoll. Allerdings müßte man beachten, daß das Bild von Bauwerken oder architektonischen Situationen nicht rund und nicht komplex sein wird, wenn man es nur unter diesem einen Aspekt sehen würde. Dennoch lohnt es sich.»[27]

Stets wird nach neuen Verbindungen und neuen Möglichkeiten aller Art gesucht, und es verwundert kaum, daß Behnisch sich mit den gegenwärtig in Berlin so gefragten neohistoristischen Natursteinfassaden nicht zu identifizieren vermag. Seiner Ansicht nach befindet sich die Glasfassade noch im Entwicklungsstadium; man ist immer noch dabei, das ganze komplexe Potential der Reflexion und Refraktion des Lichtes zu entdecken, die neue Art der Beziehungen zwischen innen und außen. Die Architektur könnte – und sollte – diese neuen Möglichkeiten ausloten. Sie sollte es, weil uns die alten Wege verschlossen sind und Schönheit nicht mehr unter dem Zeichen verlorengegangener Meisterschaft zu erzielen ist. Die neue Akademie der Künste (S. 119) ist ein eng von der Nachbarbebauung umschlossenes öffentliches Gebäude, das einer festen Beziehung zur Straße bedarf, denn es muß sich im öffentlichen Bereich darstellen, und seine Räume müssen nach außen orientiert sein. Behnisch akzeptierte die Voraussetzung, daß der Platz in seiner früheren Form bebaut würde, integrierte die erhaltenen Ausstellungssäle und übernahm sogar den Rhythmus und die Proportionen der alten Fassade, lehnte jedoch die Vorstellung, daß die neue Ansicht aus einer massiven Wand mit Fensterhöhlen bestehen sollte, als anachronistisch ab. Es gab lange Diskussionen, an deren Ende das Gebäude schließ-

rectional red spar (p. 106) to the intentionally ship-like image of the Luginsland Kindergarten (p. 90). Applied colour has been used increasingly, speculated about and refined: here the talents of Christian Kandzia come particularly to the fore,[25] but specialist artists have also been commissioned.[26] The following comment by Behnisch shows how seriously colour should be taken, not as trivial decoration but as a symptom of far deeper issues:
"By adding colour, I try to overcome the pre-ordained world. The world in question is not only the world of appearances. Often, I want to overcome a world dominated by certain forces, e. g. of production, marketing, administration systems. These systems urge me to use products that are cheap and clever and perhaps also durable. But I dislike them. I want to keep my distance from them. And I do not want the objects of this world to be visible around me. They are welcome as invisible assistants – as assistants who, wherever they appear in my image of the world, have to wear beautiful garments, like courtiers had to in the past... More attention should be given to colour. It costs little; it is unfettered and effective. It has to be borne in mind that the visual impact of buildings or architectural contexts will not be complete or complex if it is considered from this context alone. But it is nonetheless worthwhile."[27]

New relationships and new possibilities of all kinds are always being sought, and it is scarcely surprising that Behnisch felt unable to conform with the neo-historicist stone facades currently demanded in Berlin. As he sees it, the glass-facade is still under development, we are still discovering the complex possibilities of reflection and refraction, the new kind of relationships that can be made between inside and out. Architecture can – and should – explore these new possibilities. It should because the old ways are closed to us, and beauty can no longer reside in the signature of a vanished craftsmanship. The new Akademie der Künste (p. 119) is a public building tightly hemmed in by neighbours that needs a strong relationship with the street, for its rooms must look out and it needs to be represented in the public realm. Behnisch ac-

lich akzeptiert wurde. Behnisch verwunderte die Aufregung über eine nur 36 m lange Fassade; das Projekt wurde jedoch zum Testfall für die Planungsvorstellungen in der Hauptstadt. Ein Architekt von seinem Rang und politischen Bewußtsein war notwendig, um den Weg zu weisen, um die Berliner daran zu erinnern, daß wir für die Zukunft bauen, zugleich aber die Erinnerung an das Vergangene bewahren sollen und daß ein sensibles Interpretieren der Situation niemals durch strenge und festgelegte Regeln ersetzt werden kann.[28]

Der Aufbau des Buches
Weil es einfacher ist, Ähnliches miteinander zu vergleichen, werden die Bauten und Projekte in diesem Buch in Gruppen nach Typen präsentiert, wobei letztere so zusammengestellt sind, daß sie eine erzählende Folge bilden. Zuerst kommen *Schulbauten*, der umfassendste Typ in Behnischs Werk, mit Beispielen aus jedem Stadium der Entwicklung des Büros, vor allem der frühen Jahre. Die Kommentare können unabhängig voneinander oder als Folge gelesen werden, um den sich wandelnden Charakter und die Entwicklung von Ideen nachzuvollziehen. Der nächste Abschnitt, *Sportbauten*, enthält den bedeutenden Olympiapark, aber auch einige Schulsporthallen. Die damit verbundenen großen Spannweiten erforderten die Betonung ingenieurbautechnischer Fragen, daher repräsentieren diese Bauten sehr deutlich den Wandel in den Beziehungen zwischen architektonischer Ordnung und tektonischen Belangen. Der darauffolgende Abschnitt, *Sozialbauten*, enthält Seniorenheime, Kindergärten und das einzige Projekt des Büros für sozialen Wohnungsbau, das kürzlich fertiggestellt wurde. *Kulturbauten* behandelt Museen und Bibliotheken, von denen das Frankfurter Postmuseum ein bemerkenswertes Beispiel für «Situationsarchitektur» bildet. *Verwaltungs- und Industriebauten* zeigt Bürogebäude und Fabriken. Darunter fallen der berühmte Bau für das Diakonische Werk, der eine neue Richtung im Bürobau begründete, und das riesige Gebäude der Baden-Württembergischen Landesbank, Behnischs wichtigstes innerstädtisches Bauwerk. Das kurze Kapitel *Verkehrsbauten* enthält Straßenbahn-, Bus- und U-Bahn-Stationen in Stuttgart sowie den Kontrollturm des Flughafens Nürnberg, während der Abschnitt *Bundesbauten* die verschiedenen Stadien der Bonner Parlamentsbauten vorstellt, des langwierigsten und, vielleicht vom Olympiapark abgesehen, bedeutendsten Auftrags, den das Büro Behnisch bisher ausgeführt hat.

[1] Im Gegensatz etwa zu Richard Meier oder Zaha Hadid, die einen persönlichen Stil entwickelt haben, der ablesbar und übertragbar ist. Selbst bei Architekten, die eine beachtliche Vielfalt von Formensprachen

cepted the principle that the square be rebuilt in its former position, incorporated the surviving exhibition halls, and even adopted the rhythm and proportions of the old facade, but he rejected as anachronistic the idea that the facade should be a solid wall with window-holes. There were long arguments, but in the end the building was accepted, though it still awaits funding. Behnisch was surprised about the fuss over a mere 36 m length of facade, but it became an important test-case for planning attitudes in the capital. An architect of his stature and political awareness was needed to show the way forward, to remind Berliners that we build for the future as well as preserving the memory of the past, and that sensitive interpretation of the situation can never be replaced by hard and fast rules.[28]

Structure of the book
Because it is easier to compare like with like, the buildings and projects are presented in groups according to type, with the types arranged to produce a narrative progression. First come *Educational Buildings*, the most numerous type in the Behnisch oeuvre, with examples from every stage in the firm's development, especially the early years. The commentaries can be looked at independently or read in sequence to show the changing character and unfolding ideas in the work. The subsequent section, *Buildings for Sport*, includes the important Olympic Park, but also some school sports-halls. The large spans involved put the accent on engineering, so these buildings demonstrate more clearly the changing relationship between architectural ordering and tectonic concerns. The following section, *Social Buildings*, covers old people's homes, kindergartens and the one social housing project recently undertaken by the firm. *Cultural Buildings* deals with museums and libraries, the Frankfurt Postmuseum being a noteworthy example of "Situationsarchitektur". *Commercial Buildings* deals with offices and factories. It contains both the famous Diakonie which started a new line in office developments and the huge Landesgirokasse bank, Behnisch's most important urban building. The short section *Buildings for Transport* contains the tram, bus and underground stations around Stuttgart and the Nuremberg airport control tower, while the section *Political Buildings* covers the various stages of the new Parliament at Bonn, the Behnisch office's longest and, with the possible exception of the Olympic Park, most prestigious commission.

[1] In comparison, for example with Richard Meier or Zaha Hadid, who have produced a personal style that can be recognised and bought. Even when there is considerable variety in style, as for example with the

work of James Stirling, the signature can still be present. A telling example in this case was the presentation of Stirling's accumulated work in a kind of ideal city for "Roma Interrotta".

2 When I asked Behnisch about this, he claimed that if he took up the pencil the others would all stop and watch. He therefore resists the temptation.

3 Think of Mies van der Rohe, Le Corbusier or Frank Lloyd Wright, but this is not only a 20th century problem. In his biography *Philip Webb and his work*, W. R. Lethaby quotes Webb on his time at G. E. Street's office: "Street would not let us design a keyhole."

4 People in the Behnisch office remarked to me more than once that although the Hysolar building shows the influence of Coop Himmelblau, the project architect being Frank Stepper who had worked for them, Behnisch's office was needed to get such a thing built, both in terms of getting the ideas accepted and in terms of technical backup.

5 For example, the main stair at the Post museum was widened in the secondary construction after the concrete was cast, because though looking acceptable on plan it seemed too mean in reality.

6 The two partners of Auer + Weber were both for a time partners in the Behnisch firm. Equally important for the current German scene are Kauffmann & Theilig and Herrmann + Bosch.

7 All this and much subsequent information from a series of taped interviews by the author with Günter Behnisch in September 1998.

8 "In its campaign to repress the whole way of thinking engendered by the movement for New Building, the Third Reich has succeeded in rendering it quite unknown... The movement needs almost to start again from scratch, and today it faces greater obstacles than at the turn of the century, for the cultural prejudices of the Third Reich have engendered a deep enmity for all intellectual movements... The National Socialist conception of building still has exclusive command of the field here... We architects of New Building must unite in solidarity and understanding... to make sure that at least the next generation comes to some kind of fruition." Extract from a circular letter by Hugo Häring dated 24 September 1948; from a copy in the Lauterbach Archive, Akademie der Künste, Berlin: translation.

9 Heinrich Lauterbach was an architect from Breslau involved in the modernist circle of Scharoun and Rading, professors at the Kunstakademie from 1925–32. He was the organiser of the Breslau Werkbund Exhibition in 1929, and his House Hasek in Gablonz of 1931 earned a prominent place in F. R. S.

9 Heinrich Lauterbach war Architekt in Breslau und mit dem Kreis moderner Architekten um Scharoun und Rading verbunden, die von 1925 bis 1932 an der dortigen Kunstakademie lehrten. Er war auch der Organisator der Breslauer Werkbund-Ausstellung von 1929, und sein Haus Hasek in Gablonz von 1931 erhielt einen bevorzugten Platz in F. R. S. Yorkes Buch *The Modern House*. In den fünfziger Jahren zog Lauterbach nach Kassel, wo er ein kleines Büro unterhielt, und gab dann mit Jürgen Joedicke die erste Monographie über Hugo Häring heraus, die 1965 im Verlag Karl Krämer, Stuttgart, veröffentlicht wurde.

10 Frank Lloyd Wright, der sein ganzes Leben lang konsequent den Begriff «organische Architektur» benutzte, definierte sie einmal als «die Sache, die aus der Natur der Sache entsteht», und Hugo Häring, der führende Theoretiker der organischen Richtung in Deutschland, beschloß seinen Grundsatzbeitrag *wege zur form*, 1925, mit den Worten: «Nicht unsere individualität haben wir zu gestalten, sondern die individualität der dinge. Ihr ausdruck sei identisch mit ihnen selbst.» Die maßgebliche Geschichte der frühen organischen Architektur ist Bruno Zevis *Towards an Organic Architecture*, Faber and Faber, London 1949. Zu Härings Theorien siehe mein Buch *Hugo Häring: the organic versus the geometric*, Edition Axel Menges, Stuttgart 1999.

11 Die in dieser Zeit entstandenen Bauten wurden jedoch Behnisch und dem ausführenden Architekten zugeschrieben.

12 Siehe Andrew Saint, *Towards a social architecture* über die Richtung der Hertfordshire Schools in England und auch Gilbert Herbert, *The dream of the factory-made house*, MIT Press, Cambridge/Mass. 1984.

13 Die besten allgemeinen Texte über Behnischs vorfabrizierten Systeme sind Günter Behnisch, *Erfahrungen beim Bauen mit Stahlbetonfertigteilen im Schulbau*, in: *Bauen + Wohnen*, September 1964, S. 361–380, und Erhard Tränkner, *Die Anforderung an den Architekten beim Fertigteilbau im Vergleich zu den Anforderungen in der herkömmlichen Bauweise*, in: Zeitschrift *Fertigteilbau*.

14 Aus: *Das Neue ist nicht das Alte*, Beitrag von Günter Behnisch in: *deutsche bauzeitung*, September 1987, S. 32–39.

15 Siehe *Skulptur und Macht*, Katalog der Ausstellung an der Akademie der Künste, Berlin, Mai–Juli 1983.

16 Der Beitrag des Landschaftsarchitekten Günther Grzimek war von zentraler Bedeutung, auch wenn er nicht am Wettbewerbsentwurf beteiligt gewesen war. Obgleich das Landschaftskonzept beschlossen worden

Yorke's *The Modern House*. In the 1950s Lauterbach moved to Kassel where he continued to practice in a small way, and he became co-editor with Jürgen Joedicke of the first monograph on Hugo Häring, published by Karl Krämer, Stuttgart, in 1965.

10 Frank Lloyd Wright, who consistently used the term Organic Architecture through out his life, once defined it as "the thing growing out of the nature of the thing" and Hugo Häring, the leading theorist of the organic direction in Germany ended his key essay *wege zur form*, 1925, with the comment: "it is not our own individuality that we should express, but the individuality of things: their expression should be identical with their being" (my translation). The classic early history of organic architecture is Bruno Zevi's *Towards an Organic Architecture*, Faber and Faber, London, 1949. For Häring's theories see my *Hugo Häring: the organic versus the geometric*, Edition Axel Menges 1999.

11 But the buildings at this time were credited to Behnisch and the job architect concerned.

12 See Andrew Saint *Towards a social architecture*, about the Hertfordshire Schools movement in Britain, and also Gilbert Herbert *The dream of the factory-made house*, MIT Press, Cambridge, Mass. 1984.

13 The best general texts on the Behnisch prefabricated systems are Günter Behnisch *Erfahrungen beim Bauen mit Stahlbetonfertigteilen im Schulbau,* published in *Bauen + Wohnen,* September 1964, p 361–380; and Erhard Tränkner *Die Anforderungen an den Architekten beim Fertigteilbau im Vergleich zu den Anforderungen in der herkömmlichen Bauweise*, published in the periodical *Fertigteilbau*.

14 From *Das Neue ist nicht das Alte*, signed article by Günter Behnisch, *deutsche bauzeitung* September 1987, p 32–39.

15 See *Skulptur und Macht*, catalogue of the exhibition at the Akademie der Künste, Berlin, of May-July 1983.

16 Landscape architect Günther Grzimek's contribution was of central importance even though he had not been involved in the competition proposal. Although the concept for the landscape had been decided before he came on the scene, the dominant role given to the landscape and its intimate relationship with the buildings was for Grzimek unusual and highly welcome. As he wrote in his catalogue essay: "Seldom has any work given me such pleasure as the design of the Olympic Park." *Behnisch & Partner. Bauten 1952–1992,* Gert Hatje, Stuttgart 1992, p 33.

17 As Behnisch commented in 1992: "The competition came for us at just the right time. We were well pre-

war, noch ehe er einbezogen wurde, waren die der Landschaft zugewiesene beherrschende Rolle und ihre enge Beziehung zu den Bauten für Grzimek ungewöhnlich und hochwillkommen. In seinem Beitrag zum Katalog schrieb er: «Selten hat mir eine Arbeit soviel Spaß gemacht wie die Gestaltung des Olympiaparks in München.» *Behnisch & Partner. Bauten 1952–1992*, Verlag Gerd Hatje, Stuttgart 1992, S. 33.

17 Behnisch kommentierte dies 1992 wie folgt: «Für uns kam dieser Wettbewerb zur rechten Zeit: Wir hatten unsere Fertigkeiten gut ausgebildet und hatten uns gelöst von strengen formalen Ordnungen. Wir hatten erfahren, wie vorsichtig wir mit dem gesamten Material von Architektur umgehen sollten, welch große Kräfte im Wesen der Dinge stecken können und daß wir offen und fair sein müssen, auch den Dingen gegenüber.» *Behnisch & Partner*, a. a. O., S. 71.

18 Zur Schilderung der ingenieurmäßigen Entwicklung und der Rolle der verschiedenen beteiligten Personen siehe Alan Holgate, *The Art of Structural Engineering, the Work of Jörg Schlaich and his Team*, Edition Axel Menges, Stuttgart 1997, S. 64–75.

19 Günter Behnisch, Ansprache zur Eröffnung der Eiermann-Ausstellung, München 1984/85, unveröffentlichtes Typoskript.

20 Duikers einflußreichste Bauten waren das Sanatorium Zonnestraal in Hilversum von 1925–1928 und die Freiluftschule in Amsterdam von 1927/28. Sein Werk ist bemerkenswert wegen des subtilen Zusammenspiels von Glashaut und Betonskelett.

21 Behnisch in der Broschüre zur Eröffnung des Gebäudes 1979: *Haus Birkach. Studienzentrum der Evangelischen Landeskirche in Württemberg.*

22 Siehe den Grundsatzbeitrag von Häring *wege zur form* von 1925, in: Joedicke/Lauterbach, *Hugo Häring*, Karl Krämer Verlag, Stuttgart 1965.

23 Zu weiteren Informationen über Scharoun siehe Peter Blundell Jones, *Hans Scharoun*, Phaidon, London 1995.

24 «Das Formale ist frei», Interview mit dem Autor, 1991.

25 Kandzia ist seit 1969 im Büro. Heute ist er Seniorarchitekt, Fotograf, Archivar und betreut das Finish der Bauten.

26 Fritz Fuchs in Stuttgart-Birkach, Nicola de Maria in Bonn (Abgeordnetenrestaurant), Erich Wiesner in Öhringen, Dresden und Bad Elster.

27 Aus Behnischs Broschüre *Über das Farbliche/On Colour*, Verlag Gerd Hatje, Stuttgart 1993.

28 Behnisch hat ein kleines Buch verfaßt über seinen Kampf um die Akzeptanz dieses Gebäudes: *Der Pariser Platz: die Akademie der Künste*, Jovis, Berlin 1997.

pared and had freed ourselves from strong formal ordering systems. We had experienced just how carefully the whole substance of architecture has to be handled and how easily it can be dominated and thrown off balance by certain forces. We had understood that we must take a fair and open attitude not only to people but also to things." Günter Behnisch quoted from *Behnisch & Partner,* 1992, op. cit., p 71: my translation.

18 For a clear narrative of the engineering development and the roles of the various personalities involved see Alan Holgate *The Art of Structural Engineering, the Work of Jörg Schlaich and his Team,* Edition Axel Menges, Stuttgart 1997, p 64–75.

19 Behnisch, address at the opening of the Eiermann Exhibition, Munich, 1984/5. Unpublished typescript supplied by him. My translation.

20 Duiker's most influential buildings were the Zonnestraal Sanatorium Hilversum of 1925–28 and the open-air school, Amsterdam, of 1927/8. The work is notable for its subtle interplay of glass skin and concrete bones.

21 Behnisch in the brochure for the opening of the building in 1979, quoted in Dominique Gauzin-Müller *Behnisch & Partners. 50 years of architecture,* Academy Editions, London 1997, p 91.

22 See the key essay by Häring *wege zur form* of 1925, printed in German in Joedicke/Lauterbach *Hugo Häring,* Karl Krämer, Stuttgart 1965, in English in the Open University source-book *Form and Function* edited by Benton and Sharp.

23 For more information on Scharoun, see Peter Blundell Jones *Hans Scharoun*, Phaidon, London 1995.

24 "Das Formale ist Frei", interview with the author, 1991.

25 Kandzia has been with the office since 1969. He is senior architect, photographer, archivist, and the supervisor of buildings in their final stages.

26 Fritz Fuchs in Stuttgart-Birkach, Nicola De Maria at Bonn (restaurant for members of parliament), Erich Wiesner at Öhringen, Dresden and Bad Elster.

27 From Behnisch's booklet *On colour*, published by Gerd Hatje, Stuttgart 1993.

28 Behnisch wrote a booklet about the struggle to get this building accepted, published by Jovis, Berlin under the title *Der Pariser Platz: die Akademie der Künste,* 1997.

Alle Grundrisse sind nach Norden ausgerichtet.

All floor plans are oriented to the north.

Bauten und Projekte   Buildings and Projects

Schulbauten

Hohenstaufen-Gymnasium
Göppingen, 1959
Mit Bruno Lambart

Ein viergeschossiger, linearer Klassentrakt ist mit zwei kürzeren, beidseitig parallel zu ihm gestellten zweigeschossigen Flügeln verbunden. Diese Nebentrakte enthalten Spezialklassen für Kunst und Naturwissenschaften. Vom Hauptblock sind sie auf zwei Ebenen durch verglaste Korridore erschlossen und umgrenzen einen geschützten Innenhof, der einem Kreuzgang ähnelt und als Freibereich für Versammlungen genutzt wird. Diese Schule ist, obgleich überwiegend aus Ortbeton errichtet, weitgehend standardisiert und streng orthogonal; sie spiegelt die damals vorherrschende Überzeugung von der Wirtschaftlichkeit der Serienfertigung und etablierte eine Architektursprache, wie sie bei vielen vorfabrizierten Schulen der Folgezeit verwendet wurde. Zu beachten ist die frühe Horizontalgliederung der Südfassaden durch Sonnenschutzelemente (inzwischen demontiert durch Architekten der Stadt Göppingen).

Educational Buildings

Hohenstaufen grammar school
Göppingen, 1959
With Bruno Lambart

A four-storey linear classroom block is combined with a pair of shorter two-storey wings placed parallel, one on each side. These satellite wings contain specialised teaching rooms for arts and sciences. They are linked to the main block by glazed corridors at two levels, enclosing a sheltered cloister-like court to be used for outdoor assemblies. Although made largely of concrete cast in-situ, this school is highly standardised and strictly orthogonal, reflecting the prevailing contemporary belief in the economy of the series. It establishes the kind of architectural language that was to be used in many prefabricated schools to follow. Note the early layering of south facades with sun-shading devices (since removed by local authority architects).

Innenhof
Inner courtyard

Lageplan
Site plan

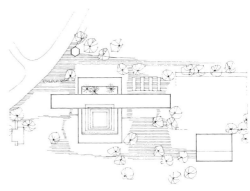

Ansicht von Westen. Relief von Fritz Nuß / View from the west. Relief by Fritz Nuß

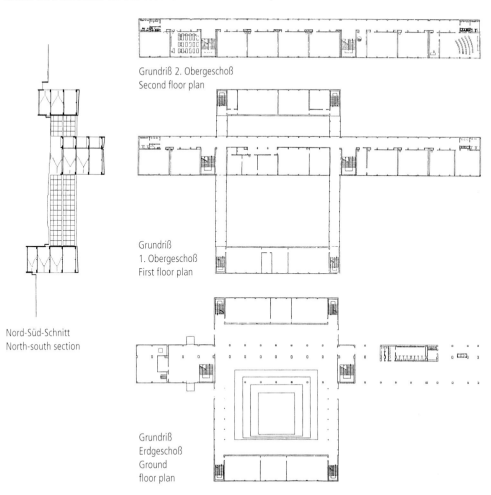

Grundriß 2. Obergeschoß
Second floor plan

Grundriß
1. Obergeschoß
First floor plan

Nord-Süd-Schnitt
North-south section

Grundriß
Erdgeschoß
Ground
floor plan

Vogelsangschule
Stuttgart, 1961
Mit Bruno Lambart

Diese Schule folgt einer internationalen Bewegung, die seinerzeit die Errichtung von Pavillonschulen propagierte und in Westdeutschland von Hans Scharouns Schulbauten in Darmstadt und Lünen angeführt wurde. Die Idee war, daß jedes Kind sich mit seinem Klassenraum als zweites Zuhause identifizieren sollte. Die Klassen wurden deshalb als jeweils separates «Haus» mit eigener Garderobe gestaltet und zu dorfähnlichen Gruppen zusammengestellt. Hier ist das steil abfallende Gelände mit einem Hauptbau oben und acht paarweise angeordneten, den Abhang hinunter gestaffelten Pavillons sowie einem weiteren Gebäude bebaut, das die Turnhalle, einen Kindergarten und Sonderunterrichtsräume an der unten vorbeiführenden Straße enthält. In den Pavillons sind die beiden ersten Klassen untergebracht. Die Räume für die beiden älteren und deshalb sozial bereits besser integrierten Jahrgänge liegen, ebenso wie die Verwaltung, im Hauptbau. Die Aula ist als überdachter Innenhof ausgebildet, der von den flankierenden Klassentrakten begrenzt und durch eine große Glaswand optisch mit der Außenterrasse zusammengefaßt wird. Auffällig ist die Unterstützung des Dachfirstes mit einer freistehenden Stütze im Pausenhofbereich. Die Klassenräume sind nach Süden orientiert und mit zusätzlichen Oberlichtern versehen, was vom damals herrschenden Glauben an die gesundheitlichen Vorzüge des Sonnenlichts zeugt. Die Konstruktion besteht aus rotem Backstein und Ortbeton mit flach geneigten Bitumendächern.

Vogelsang school
Stuttgart, 1961
With Bruno Lambart

This school belongs to an international movement in pavilion schools, led in Germany by Hans Scharoun with his Darmstadt and Lünen schools. The idea was that the child should identify with the class as a second home, which should therefore be presented as a separate "house" with its own cloakroom, contributing to a village-like group. Here the steeply sloping site is developed with a main building at the top, eight pavilions linked in pairs tumbling down the slope, and a further building containing a gymnasium, a kindergarten and specialised classrooms next to the lower street. The pavilions house classes for children of the first two years. Classrooms for the two older years, whose social integration is already more complete, are grouped with the administration in the main building. The assembly hall is treated as a roofed cour tenclosed by the flanking classroom tracts, and is made visually continuous with the main terrace outside by a huge glass wall. The roof is supported on a single column – a bold move for the time. Classrooms face south with additional clerestorey glazing, reflecting a prevailing belief in the health benefits of sunlight. Construction is red brick and in-situ concrete with shallow-pitched felted roofs.

Grundriß der Schulanlage mit Turnhalle / Plan of school grounds with gymnasium

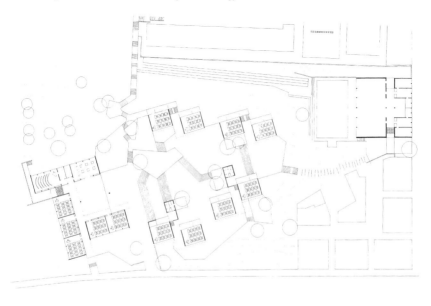

Klassenpavillons und Hauptbau / Classroom pavilions and main building

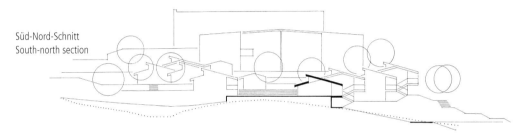

Süd-Nord-Schnitt
South-north section

Klassenpavillons am Pausenhof / Classroom pavilions along schoolyard

Fachhochschule/Hochschule für Technik
Ulm, 1963, Erweiterung 1985

Dieser preisgekrönte Wettbewerbsentwurf von 1959 ist zum Prototyp für ein Fertigteil-Bausystem aus Beton geworden. Es wurde in Zusammenarbeit mit der Firma Rostan entwickelt und ließ sich mit Ausnahme der Fundamente fast überall verwenden. Der Konstruktion liegt ein Raster von 3 × 3 m zugrunde; Behnisch bemühte sich jedoch, die Strenge des Systems zu mildern, indem er die Bauelemente soweit wie möglich variierte. Er nutzte auch die Vorzüge des Baugeländes, einer alten Festungsanlage am Stadtrand von Ulm, das eine großartige Aussicht bietet und die Möglichkeit, die Ebenen des Gebäudes dem fallenden Gelände anzupassen. Zwei viergeschossige Seminarbauten sind westöstlich gestellt und mit niedrigeren Trakten verbunden, so daß sich eine Raumfolge ergibt. Die wichtigsten Außenräume bilden ein kleiner, kreuzgangähnlicher Hof zwischen den Laboratorien und ein größerer Eingangshof. Da der nördliche Seminarbau ein Geschoß höher auf den Boden trifft als der südliche, konnte eine Verbindung auf dem Niveau des ersten Obergeschosses hergestellt und der größere Innenhof durch Stufen terrassiert werden. Wer auf der unteren Ebene eintritt, wendet sich vom Hof nach rechts einem eindrucksvollen Architekturbereich zu: der langgestreckten, verglasten Halle des südlichen Traktes. Sie wird rhythmisch gegliedert durch die Treppen zu den oberen Ebenen und verbindet die Aula an der Südwestecke mit dem zentralen Komplex. Die subtile Wechselwirkung des Raumes bildet ein Gegengewicht zur Starrheit des Systems, dessen Strenge der zeitgenössischen Auffassung entsprach. Selten wurden Fertigbausysteme so phantasievoll eingesetzt.

Ulm engineering school
1963, extended 1985

This winning competition design of 1959 became the prototype for a precast concrete building system. Developed in collaboration with the firm Rostan, it was used for almost everything except foundations. A construction grid of 3 × 3 m was imposed, but Behnisch strove to alleviate the rigidity of the system by varying the building elements as much as possible. Good use was also made of the site, an old fortification at the edge of Ulm which offered spectacular views and changes of level. Two four-storey classroom blocks run west-east across the site, linked with lower structures to define a sequence of spaces. The main external rooms are two courts, one small and cloister-like between the laboratories, the other a larger entry court. Since the north classroom block joins the ground one storey higher than the south, a connection could be made at first floor level, and the larger court is terraced with steps. Those entering at lower ground level turn right from the court to encounter the most architecturally exciting space: a long glazed concourse between the columns of the southern block.
Punctuated rhythmically by stairs to upper levels, it links the main lecture hall at the south-east corner to the heart of the complex. The subtle interplay of space relieves the rigidity of the system, whose austerity reflects the attitudes of the period. Prefabricated building systems were seldom deployed so imaginatively.

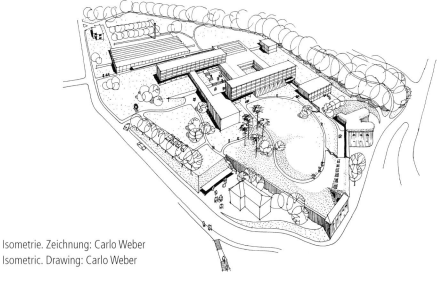

Isometrie. Zeichnung: Carlo Weber
Isometric. Drawing: Carlo Weber

Beispiel einer Montageschule
Fa. Rostan, System Behnisch
Example of a prefabricated
school Rostan Company,
Behnisch system

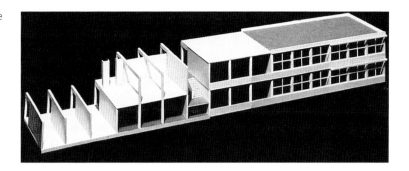

Grundriß Hauptgeschoß mit
Einzellaboratien (oben) und
Hauptbau
Plan of main floor with
individual laboratories
(above) and main building

Längsschnitt Nord-Süd
Longitudinal section
north-south

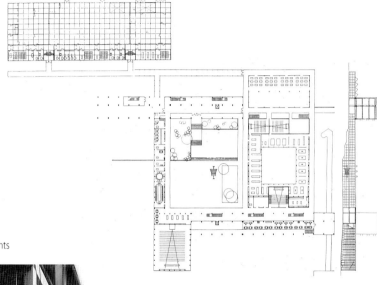

Montage der Fertigteile
Assembly of prefabricated elements

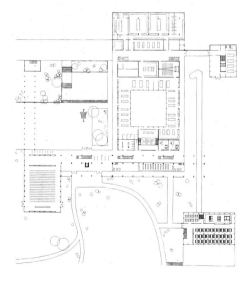

Grundriß Erdgeschoß Hauptbau
Ground floor plan of main building

Ansicht Seminarbau Süd und Aula / View of southern seminar building and assembly hall

Halle Süd
South hall

Progymnasium
jetzt Hauptschule
Furtwangen, 1965

Grammar school
now secondary modern school
Furtwangen, 1965

Die hoch an einen stark abfallenden Schwarzwaldhang gesetzten, horizontal ausladenden Ebenen sind stufenförmig nach oben angeordnet, so daß eine Folge von ostorientierten Terrassen entsteht. Die eindrucksvollen Treppenläufe führen entlang dem zentralen Kern und verbinden die auf beiden Seiten überwiegend einzelne Klassenräume enthaltenden Geschosse; nur die unterste Ebene ist zwischen den Stützen zur Erweiterung der Pausenhalle freigelassen. Die ausgesetzte Lage und die schwierigen Klimabedingungen im Schwarzwald beschränkten die Bautätigkeit auf den Sommer, so daß eine kurze Bauzeit von besonderem Vorteil war. Wenngleich die monotone Aneinanderreihung von Elementen durch den interessanten Schnitt und das Wechselspiel der Innenräume etwas aufgelockert wurde, konnte sie nicht genügend ausgeglichen werden, und Behnisch gab diese Bauweise bald danach auf.

Perched high on a Black Forest hillside, the slab-like floors step up the slope to leave a series of east-facing roof terraces. Staircases run dramatically along the central spine linking the floors, which are mostly divided into separate classrooms on each side, but the lowest floor is left open between the columns to enlarge the assembly hall. The exposure of the situation limited building to the summer, so speed of erection was of particular advantage. Though it is somewhat relieved by the exciting section and the play with internal spaces, the dumb repetition of components could not be adequately mitigated, and Behnisch abandoned this approach soon afterwards.

West-Ost-Schnitt
West-east section

Grundriß Eingangsebene
Entrance level plan

Grundriß 1. Obergeschoß
First floor plan

Südseite / South side

Nachbarschaftsschule «In den Berglen»
Berglen-Oppelsbohm, 1969

Dieses Projekt bezeichnet einen Wendepunkt; es beendete die Periode der Standardisierung und Vorfabrikation und ebnete den Weg zu immer freieren Lösungen. Alle Klassenräume haben dieselbe fünfeckige Form, sind im gleichen Winkel angeordnet, und ihre Fassaden sind exakt modular, der Grundriß ist jedoch konzentrisch – ein begrenztes und hierarchisch zentriertes System, ganz im Gegensatz zur abstrakten Neutralität des Rasters. Ausschlaggebend war der Wunsch nach Flexibilität, daher die teilbaren und kombinierbaren Bereiche; aber der polygonale Grundriß erwies sich auch als geeignet für eine andere Nutzung des Raumes. An die Stelle der Flure trat die zentrale Halle, die für Zusammenkünfte wie auch als Verkehrsbereich dient. Das «Sichversammeln als Gesellschaft», die sich dann in getrennte Gruppen an der Peripherie auflöst, ist räumlich auf ganz direkte Weise dargestellt. Jeder Klassenraum hat seine individuelle Orientierung und Aussicht zur landschaftlich reizvollen Umgebung. Die innerhalb der polygonalen Grundrißgeometrie frei an den Hang gesetzte Schule wird von unten über eine offene Pausenhalle betreten, die einen geschützten Schwellenbereich bildet. Die frei in die Halle eingefügten Treppen führen eine neue räumliche Dynamik ein, die in späteren Werken weiterentwickelt wurde.

"In den Berglen" school
Berglen-Oppelsbohm, 1969

This project marks a turning point, ending the period of modularisation and prefabrication and opening the way for an increasingly freer approach. The classrooms – they are all pentagonal – repeat the same angle and their facades are precisely modular but the layout is concentric, a finite and hierarchically focused system as opposed to the abstract neutrality of the grid. The starting point was a concern for flexibility, hence the divisible and combinable areas, but the polygonal plan also proved efficient in the use of space, replacing corridors with a central hall to serve both for assembly and circulation. Coming together as a whole society then dispersing to separate groups on the periphery is presented spatially in the most direct way. Each classroom has its own special orientation and view of the beautiful surrounding landscape. Set into the side of the hill, the school is entered from below, between the supporting columns which provide a sheltered threshold. The independent placing of staircases within the hall necessitated by the polygonal plan geometry introduced a new spatial dynamic further exploited in later work.

Ansicht von Süden / View from the south

Halle / Hall

Isometrie
Isometric

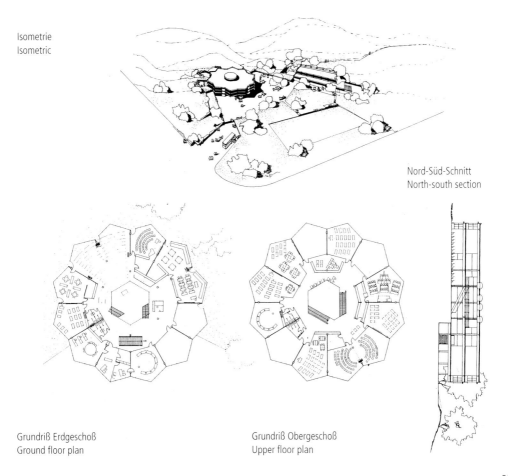

Nord-Süd-Schnitt
North-south section

Grundriß Erdgeschoß
Ground floor plan

Grundriß Obergeschoß
Upper floor plan

Progymnasium auf dem Schäfersfeld
Lorch, 1973, Erweiterung 1994

Das malerische Städtchen Lorch ist in ein von kleinen Hügeln umgebenes Tal eingebettet und wird von zwei natürlichen Höhenzügen überragt: Auf dem einen steht ein romanisches Kloster, auf dem anderen der Schulkomplex von Behnisch. Zuerst wurde 1973 das Progymnasium errichtet, 1976 gefolgt von der Sporthalle (S. 76) und 1982 von der Hauptschule (S. 48).
Das Progymnasium nimmt den polygonalen Grundriß der Oppelsbohmer Schule (S. 34) auf, verwendet ihn jedoch nur beim Klassentrakt der oberen Ebenen. Im Hauptgeschoß sind einzelne Flügel angefügt und bilden ablesbare Bereiche für Spezialklassen: Naturwissenschaften auf der einen, Kunst und Werken auf der anderen Seite, dazwischen Eingang und Verwaltung. Die von allen genutzte Halle im Zentrum des Klassentraktes bildet auch hier den eindeutigen Mittelpunkt; strenge geometrische Begrenzungen sind jedoch aufgehoben, um den Raum leichter zugänglich zu machen. Die runde Treppenhalle wurde aus der Mitte verschoben, um Platz für den Versammlungsbereich vor den Klassenräumen im Hauptgeschoß zu schaffen. Dort ist die Zentralorientierung ganz aufgehoben. Ein zweites Wegesystem erlaubt Ausblick durch Glaswände und -türen auf den umgebenden Garten. Der größere Seitenflügel umschließt ein fünfeckiges Glashaus (Vivarium); die Räume für den Werkunterricht strahlen von einer gemeinsamen Eingangshalle aus, die sich zum Ausstellungsbereich erweitert. Hangseitig steht die Schule auf Stützen und öffnet sich dort mit einer Pausenhalle; Stützmauern schwingen hinein. Eine zentral angeordnete Treppe führt in das Hauptgeschoß hinauf, und Glaswände begrenzen die Gemeinschaftsräume der Schüler. Die Klarheit des oberen Geschosses mit den kreisförmig angeordneten Klassenräumen und zentralem, fünfeckigem Oberlicht erzeugt ein einheitliches äußeres Erscheinungsbild, dem die Nebentrakte untergeordnet sind.

Auf dem Schäfersfeld grammar school
Lorch, 1973, extended 1994

The picturesque town of Lorch nestles in a valley surrounded by small hills. It is overlooked by two natural promontories: one has a Romanesque monastery, the other Behnisch's school buildings. The grammar school of 1973 came first, followed by the sports-hall of 1976 (p. 76) and the secondary modern school of 1982 (p. 48). The grammar school repeats the polygonal plan of the Oppelsbohm school (p. 34), but uses it only for the upperfloor classroom block. In contrast, separate wings break away on the main floor to create identifiable territories for specialist subjects: science rooms one side, arts and crafts the other, with entrance and administration between. The shared hall centring the classroom block is still the main focus, but boundaries are eroded. The circular stairwell is shifted to place the assembly area next to the classrooms in the main storey. This centrality is challenged by a secondary theme of routes, with views out through glass walls and doors to gardens beyond. The larger of the side wings focuses on the pentagonal glasshouse (vivarium), and arts rooms radiate from a shared entrance hall which doubles as exhibition space. The polygonal block stands on columns to open up the lower floor to one side, and retaining walls sweep in. A centrally placed stair drops through from the floor above, and glass walls define freely-planned pupils' common rooms. The purity of the upper floor with its ring of classrooms and central pentagonal skylight creates a unified external image keeping the secondary wings subservient. Sun-shading devices added to facades reflect growing concerns with environmental control and layered facades.

Die Schulbauten auf dem Schäfersfeld und das romanische Kloster über der Stadt
Schäfersfeld school buildings and the Romanesque monastery above the town

Die zweigeschossige Halle mit Oberlicht / Double-storey hall with skylight

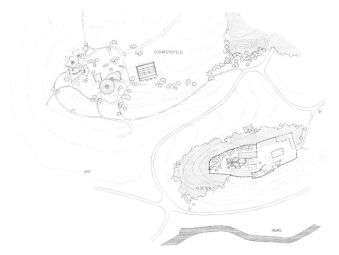

Gesamtsituation der Schul- und Sportbauten auf dem Schäfersfeld. Rechts das romanische Kloster
General situation of Schäfersfeld school and sports buildings. On the right the Romanesque monastery

Ansicht von Süd-Westen / View from the south-west

West-Ost-Schnitt
West-east section

Vivarium
Vivarium

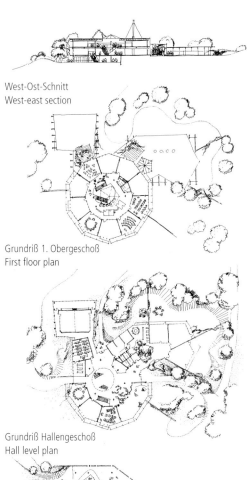

Grundriß 1. Obergeschoß
First floor plan

Grundriß Hallengeschoß
Hall level plan

Grundriß Pausenhofgeschoß
Schoolyard level plan

Klassenraum mit Erker
Classroom with bay window

Westansicht der Halle des Erweiterungsgebäudes
View from the west of the extension's hall

Naturwissenschaftlicher Bereich und Erweiterungsbau / Science area and extension

Fritz-Erler-Schule
Pforzheim, 1976

Dieser große Komplex besteht aus einem Wirtschaftsgymnasium, einer Kaufmännischen Berufsschule, einer Kaufmännischen Berufsfachschule, einer Sporthalle und einem Schwimmbad auf einem begrenzten Grundstück am Flußufer. Grundelement der Planung ist die Gruppierung von vier Klassenräumen zu einem Cluster, der jeweils einen kleinen gemeinsamen Eingangsbereich einschließt (siehe oberen Grundriß S. 42). Zwei oder drei dieser Cluster sind um eine größere gemeinsame Halle gruppiert. So entstehen drei Clustergruppen, welche die Haupteingangs- und Versammlungshalle umschließen. Die Klassenraumgruppen haben gleiche Orientierung, aber unterschiedlichen Rhythmus; die südwestliche Gruppe ist herausgerückt und enthält dadurch einen großzügigen Verkehrsbereich. Die Trakte sind auch entsprechend dem Geländeverlauf höhenversetzt. Diese Variationen führen dazu, daß jede Ecke des Erschließungssystems sich unterschiedlich einprägt und die Menschen immer wissen, wo sie sich befinden. Die zentrale Halle ist durch eine Stufenanlage gegliedert, der obere Bereich dient der Erschließung. Einige Doppelstufen sind als Sitze ausgebildet. Auf dem tieferliegenden Bereich können Aufführungen stattfinden. Die zahlreichen umlaufenden Galerien und das große Oberlicht machen diese Halle zu einem dynamischen Raum: den ersten eines in der Folgezeit von Behnisch & Partnern häufig reproduzierten Typs.

Fritz Erler school
Pforzheim, 1976

This large complex contains a commercial college, business school, business secondary school, sports hall and swimming baths on a restricted site close to the river. The key plan element is a four-classroom-group (see upper plan p. 42) with two classrooms angled, so they turn through 90° and share a short entrance hall. Paired, these groups swing through 180° to enclose a small triangular stair hall; tripled, they swing through 270° making a yet larger hall. The option of combining four in a self-contained ring is denied, for it would become too self-centred. Instead, the uncompleted figures are grouped together around a larger communal hall which serves both as entrance foyer and general assembly space. The classroom groups share a common orientation but break in rhythm, the south-west one being stepped out further to make a more generous circulation area. The blocks also step in section in response to the site. As a result of these changes, each corner of the access system is recognisably different, so people know where they are. The central hall is divided into lower and upper areas with angled steps, the upper part being reserved for circulation. Steps double as seats and focus attention on the inner corner where events can be staged. The many surrounding galleries and the great rooflight above make this a dynamic space: the first of a type often repeated by Behnisch & Partners.

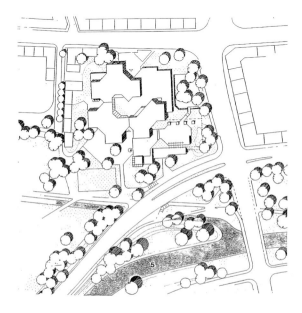

Lageplan
Site plan

Ansicht von Süden. Im Vordergrund die Enz / View from the south. In the foreground the river Enz

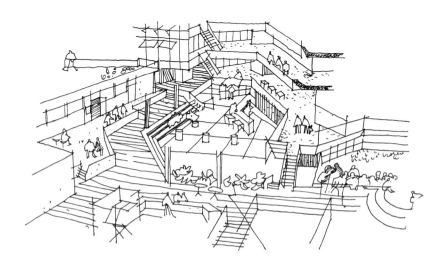

Isometrie der Halle. Zeichnung: Manfred Sabatke / Isometric of the hall. Drawing: Manfred Sabatke

Grundriß 2. Obergeschoß
Second floor plan

Offene Verbindungstreppen
Open connecting stairs

West-Ost-Schnitt
West-east section

Grundriß Eingangsebene
Entrance level plan

Grundriß untere Ebene mit
Schwimmhalle und Sporthalle
Lower level plan with indoor pool
and sports-hall

Hallenbereich unter dem Dachgarten
Hall area below the roof garden

Schwimmhalle
Indoor Pool

Luftraum der dreigeschossigen Halle
Open space of the three-storey hall

Bildungszentrum der Evangelischen Landeskirche in Württemberg
Stuttgart-Birkach, 1979

Dieses Studienzentrum der Evangelischen Landeskirche bildet fast eine Stadt für sich. Die oberen Geschosse enthalten 95 Wohnräume für Studierende, die unteren Unterrichtsräume, Büros, Bibliothek, Turnhalle und Gemeinschaftsräume. Im Wettbewerbsentwurf waren drei Ebenen terrassenartig gestaffelter Räume um einen zentralen Innenhof mit etwas starrem Grundriß gesetzt; in der gebauten Version wurde dieser jedoch aufgelockert, indem die Südseite des Innenhofes geöffnet und das Gelände dort um ein Geschoß abgesenkt wurde. Dadurch konnte die sichtbare Masse reduziert und der Eingang auf die zweite Ebene verlegt werden. Der Niveauunterschied der beiden Seiten wird beim Eintritt verständlich: Die öffentlichen Funktionen verteilen sich auf die beiden durch offene Treppen und einen Luftraum miteinander verbundenen Ebenen von Eingangs- und Gartengeschoß. Zur besseren Orientierung sind die Verkehrsbereiche durchgehend auf einer oder der anderen Seite verglast. Im Planungsverlauf entwickelten die konstituierenden Elemente zunehmend stärkere Identität. Der strenge Rhythmus der Wohnräume wird in der grau verkleideten Fassade der Obergeschosse durch kleine Erker gegliedert, während die Gemeinschaftsbereiche unten in einen größeren konstruktiven Rahmen eingebunden und überwiegend verglast sind. Der Unterrichts- und der Sporttrakt nehmen mit den ihnen eigenen funktionalen Formen und Flachdächern die beiden niedrigeren Seiten ein, während der Gemeinschaftsbereich am Eingang als geschlossene Gestalt hervortritt. Die in den Untergrund verbannten Magazine der Bibliothek sind von außen nicht ablesbar; der Lesesaal und der anschließende Gemeinschaftsbereich an der Gartenseite jedoch erhalten ihren besonderen Charakter durch die schräge Verglasung. Berechtigterweise bildet der Andachtsraum mit seiner eigenständigen Spiralform das am stärksten betonte Element und ist wie das Oratorium eines Mönchsklosters gestaltet.

Seminary Centre of the Württemberg Protestant Church
Stuttgart-Birkach, 1979

This Lutheran religious centre and residential college for priests is almost a city in itself. The upper floors contain 95 student rooms, the lower ones classrooms, offices, library, gymnasium and social rooms. The competition version wrapped three layers of terraced rooms around a central court on a somewhat rigid plan, but it was loosened up in the built version by opening the court's south side and digging it one storey into the ground. This reduces the visible bulk and effectively places the entrance at second level. The contrast in level between sides is understood on entering, for public functions are shared between the two ground floors, which are linked by open stairs and an open well. Circulation spaces are continuously glazed to one side or the other, making one's location clear. As the design developed, the constituent parts developed increasingly stronger identities. The tight rhythm of bedrooms is articulated in the grey-clad upper facade by small bay windows, while the social areas below stand within a larger structural frame and are predominantly glazed. With their own functional shapes and flat roofs, the classroom and gymnasium blocks generate the two low ends, while the community hall is articulated as a bulging form on the outside next to the entrance. Buried underneath, the book stacks of the library get no external articulation, but the reading spaces and adjacent community area on the court side gain special character from their sloping glazing. Appropriately, the most highly articulated element is the chapel, which has its own independent spiral form within the court, and is treated like an oratory within a monastic cloister.

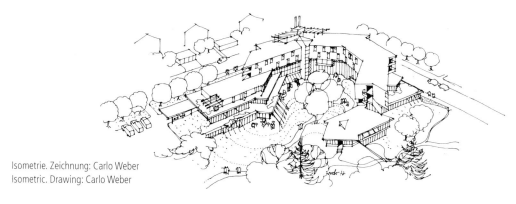

Isometrie. Zeichnung: Carlo Weber
Isometric. Drawing: Carlo Weber

Eingangshalle mit abgesenktem Gartenhof / Entrance hall with sunken garden court

Perspektive / perspective: Carlo Weber
Fassadenausschnitt Westseite / Facade detail of west side

Ansicht von Osten mit Mostbirnenbäumen / View from the east with pear trees

Gemeinschaftsbereich im Gartengeschoß
Common area on garden level

Grundriß 2. und 3. Obergeschoß
Second and third floor plan

Eingangsgeschoß
Entrance level

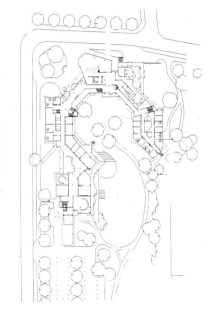

Süd-Nord-Schnitt
South-north section

Wohnzimmer
Living room

Büroraum Pfarrseminar
Office in seminary

Gartengeschoß
Garden level

Hauptschule auf dem Schäfersfeld
Lorch, 1982

Das deutsche Schulsystem ist nach Leistung aufgebaut, und zehn Jahre nach Errichtung des Progymnasiums (S. 36) benötigte Lorch eine weitere Schule ähnlicher Größe für weniger akademisch orientierte Schüler. Es war wichtig, diese Schule mit gleicher Sorgfalt zu planen, und im Rahmen der vom Büro Behnisch entwickelten Architektursprache bedeutet sie einen weiteren Schritt vorwärts. Die Klassenräume sind um eine zentrale Halle angelegt, die wie bisher als Verkehrsbereich und für Zusammenkünfte dient, aber hier dreieckig und an einer Seite zur Außenwelt geöffnet ist. An dieser verglasten Nordseite liegt auch der obere Eingang, während die spitze Ecke im Süden als bugähnlicher Abschluß der gesamten Gebäudegruppe fungiert. Zu beiden Seiten des Eingangs ragen ungleiche Trakte heraus, die, den speziellen Anforderungen der betreffenden Fächer entsprechend, Räume für Naturwissenschaften und Werken enthalten, während die hierarchisch wichtige Bugposition der Musik vorbehalten ist. Das Untergeschoß enthält auch hier wieder den Aufenthaltsbereich der Schüler sowie Räume für Kochen und textiles Werken. Behnischs vehemente Ablehnung einer Vorherrschaft der rationalen konstruktiven Ordnung zeigt sich in der zentralen Halle, die trotz ihres dreieckigen Grundrisses ein ganz ungleichmäßiges Dach hat. Eine Stahlstütze – sie betont wie eine Art Maibaum den Eingang – ist mit Rücksicht auf die Erschließung ungewöhnlich plaziert und trägt die in unterschiedlichen Winkeln geführten, verschieden langen Binder. Das konstruktive Vokabular besteht aus einer Folge sich optisch durchdringender und überschneidender Schichten, die anhand von Modellen erarbeitet wurden. Diese horizontale Schichtung löst die geometrischen Widersprüche auf praktische Weise, während ihre Präsenz sichtbar bleibt.

Auf dem Schäfersfeld secondary modern school
Lorch, 1982

The German educational system is streamed by ability, and ten years after the grammar school (p. 36) Lorch needed another school of similar size for the less academic pupils. It was important to lavish just as much care on this school, and within the Behnisch office's developing architectural language, it represents a further advance. Classrooms surround a central hall used for circulation and assembly as before, but this time it is triangular with one side open to the world beyond. This glazed north side is also the entrance, while the acute corner to south acts as a prow to terminate whole building group. On either side of the entrance erupt irregular wings of science rooms and workshops following their own logic, while the hierarchically important prow position is reserved for music. The lower floor again contains the glazed pupils' common room along with rooms for cooking and textiles. Behnisch's rebellion against the dominance of rational structural order erupts in the central hall, for though triangular in plan it has a most irregular roof. A steel column which marks the entrance like a maypole is eccentrically placed in deference to the route, and carries its radiating trusses at odd angles, each of a different length. The constructional vocabulary is developed as a series of visible overlapping and intersecting layers which were explored through physical models. This layering resolves the geometrical conflicts in a practical sense while maintaining their presence visually. Dedicated to creating the maximum social interaction, the central area of the school also displays an interaction of physical elements.

Hauptschule, Progymnasium und Sporthalle auf dem Schäfersfeld
Schäfersfeld secondary modern school, grammar school and sports-hall

Ansicht von Süd-Osten / View from the south-east

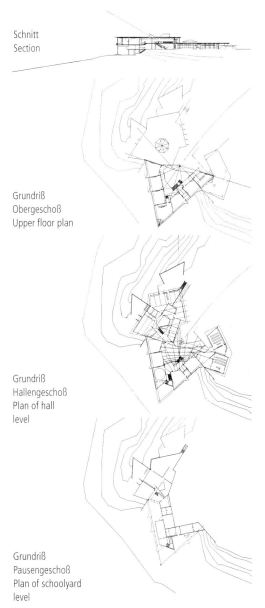

Schnitt
Section

Grundriß
Obergeschoß
Upper floor plan

Grundriß
Hallengeschoß
Plan of hall
level

Grundriß
Pausengeschoß
Plan of schoolyard
level

Klassenraum mit Erker
Classroom with bay window

Wintergarten
Winter garden

Ansicht von Nord-Osten / View from the north-east

Die Hauptschule über der Stadt Lorch / Secondary school above the town of Lorch

Die Halle mit Galerieebene / Hall with gallery level

Glasabschluß der Halle mit oberem Eingang
Glass envelope of hall with upper entrance

Albert-Schweitzer-Sonderschule
Bad Rappenau, 1991

Diese Sonderschule für lernbehinderte Kinder steht zusammen mit anderen Schulen und Sporteinrichtungen am Rande eines Wohngebiets im Baugebiet einer kleinen Stadt. Die verglaste Halle bildet ihren Schwerpunkt und zentralen Bereich: den Gemeinschaftsraum für soziale Ereignisse. Die freie Treppe darin verbindet die beiden Geschosse. Das ansteigende Gelände ermöglicht die Anordnung von Eingängen auf beiden Ebenen. Die Raumgruppen sind nach Lage und Funktion gestaltet. Der längere Trakt enthält im Obergeschoß Klassenräume, der kürzere das Lehrerzimmer und die Verwaltung. Darunter liegen, in den Hang eingebettet, eine Gruppe orthogonaler Werkstätten und Versorgungsräume. Im Gegensatz zu gewohnten Lösungen hat hier jede der beiden Ebenen ein eigenständiges Tragwerk und unterschiedliche Orientierungen: Klassenräume nach Westen, Küche und Labor nach Osten. Die schräge Plazierung der Gebäudeteile geht auf die Orientierung der benachbarten Bauten und auf die Grundstücksform zurück; die Winkel werden vorteilhaft dazu genutzt, Außenräume zu bilden und den Verkehr im Innern zu führen. Der Hauptzugang erfolgt von Südosten, wo eine durch die Baukörper gebildete Bucht als Pausenhof dient. Auf der anderen Seite umschließt der naturwissenschaftliche Trakt einen Garten mit einem biologisch angelegten Teich, Hügeln und Bäumen. Innerhalb des Gebäudes gewähren unterschiedliche Orientierungen bestmögliche Ausblicke. Die widersprüchlichen geometrischen Systeme geben die Verkehrsrichtung in der Halle an und verleihen den Klassenräumen ihren besonderen Charakter zur problemlosen Identifikation durch die Schüler. Die leicht geneigten Dächer erreichen ihren Höhepunkt über der Halle. Tages- und Sonnenlicht sind willkommen; farbenfreudige Außenjalousien entrollen sich automatisch, um ein Übermaß an Sonneneinstrahlung zu verhindern. Der gesamte Innenraum ist durch Farben hell und einladend gestaltet.

Albert Schweitzer special school
Bad Rappenau, 1991

This special school for children with learning difficulties stands among others in a small town near Heilbronn. The glazed central hall is its hub and focus; the community space for social events. Its main stair links entrances at opposite sides on different floors, taking advantage of the sloping site. Room-groups are articulated functionally and territorially. At first floor level the longer wing is classrooms, the shorter one staff room and offices. Beneath the staffrooms and set into the hill lies a group of orthogonal workshops and service rooms which constitute the building's core. In contrast, the upper classroom block influences the ground floor only through the rhythm of its structure, the other room-groups taking up new orientations: to west classrooms, to east kitchen and laboratory. The skewed placing of parts derives from the orientation of neighbouring buildings and site boundaries, the angles being used advantageously to contain space on the outside and to direct movement within. The main approach is from the south-east, where a concavity induced by the projecting wing of the science lab embraces the playground. On the opposite side, the west front embraces a garden with biological pond, mounds and trees. Within the building contrasting orientations allow exploitation of views. The conflicting geometrical systems suggest directions of movement in the hall and give the classrooms distinct characters for easy identification by pupils. Roofs are gently pitched, rising to a climax over the hall. Daylight and sun are welcomed in, with colourful external blinds unrolling automatically to reduce the excess. The interior is made bright and welcoming with applied colour.

Lageplan
Site plan

Ansicht von Nord-Westen / View from the north-west

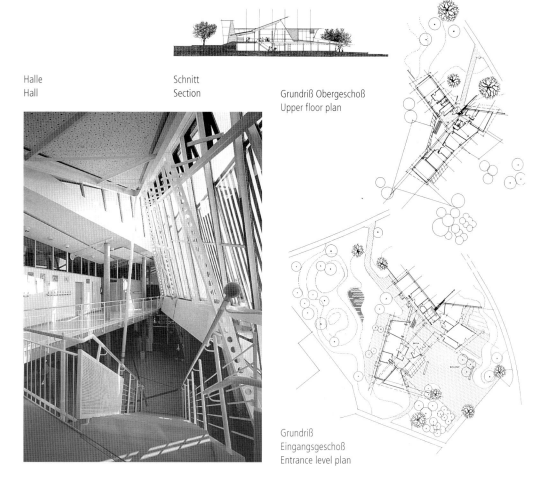

Halle
Hall

Schnitt
Section

Grundriß Obergeschoß
Upper floor plan

Grundriß
Eingangsgeschoß
Entrance level plan

Kaufmännische Schule
Öhringen, 1993

Die Schule liegt am Rande einer süddeutschen Kleinstadt, dicht an einer hohen Autobahnbrücke. Die früher liebliche ländliche Umgebung ist jetzt sporadisch mit ausufernder Vorstadtbebauung überzogen. Das Schulgebäude mußte sich nicht nur auf seinem Gelände behaupten, sondern auch ein Zeichen setzen inmitten der heterogenen Nachbarbebauung. Deshalb entstand der große, erhöht liegende Ring, der einen beträchtlichen Bereich des Grundstücks einfaßt und einen Niveauunterschied überbrückt. Die nach außen orientierten Klassenräume bieten unterschiedliche Ausblicke, während die nach innen orientierten Flure die Schüler zu einer Gemeinschaft zusammenführen. Wegen des großen Radius der Anlage können sie sich nur über den Freiraum hinweg sehen: Um sich zu treffen, müssen sie den Innengang entlang, am Haupteingang an der Südseite des Ringes vorbei zu einer dort angefügten Halle gehen. Sie dient sowohl als Foyer wie auch als Ort der Begegnung. Einige Elemente sind hervorgehoben: Hausmeisterloge, Schülerbibliothek und Cafeteria im Erdgeschoß wurden frei in die Halle eingestellt. Im oberen Geschoß liegen Verwaltung und Lehrerzimmer am Zentrum der Aktivitäten mit schönem Ausblick. In dem aufgefüllten Bereich, der wie eine Landzunge in den vom Ring gebildeten Innenraum hereinragt, sind im Nordosten die naturwissenschaftlichen Unterrichtsräume und im Nordwesten die Sporthalle eingebettet.

Farbe spielte eine wichtige Rolle. Während des Bauablaufs erkannten die Architekten in der Länge der gekrümmten Flure ein potentielles Problem und zogen den Künstler Erich Wiesner hinzu. Durch Färben der Türen und Flurtrennwände in leuchtenden Tönen reagierte er auf den unerwünschten Effekt. Behnisch kommentierte großzügig: «Wir haben nicht zum ersten Mal festgestellt, daß die Einbeziehung von «Outsidern» zwar etwas störend ist, daß sie aber auch unser Werk bereichern und uns aus unserem Trott herausholen.»

Business school
Öhringen, 1993

The school lies on the edge of a small town near Heilbronn, next to an elevated section of motorway, a once pretty rural spot now peppered with sporadic edge-city development. The building needed not only to take possession of its site, but to provide a landmark and give coherence to the neighbourhood. Hence the great raised ring, enclosing a large area of site and traversing a level change. Its extroverted classrooms face different views and orientations, while introverted corridors bring pupils together as a community. With the enormous radius they only see each other across the void: to meet they must walk around the inner passage to a triangular hall by the main entrance within the south side of the ring. This is both foyer and place of assembly. Other parts are more strongly articulated: the porter's office, pupils' library and cafeteria at ground level are set between columns and given irregular perimeters. Beyond the triangular hall on the first floor, and running out to meet the hill, are administration and staff common room: close to the centre of activities, they also have a commanding view. The tongue of elevated land running from the north into the space embraced by the school is flanked by two further elements: to north-east, half buried, a group of science rooms; to north-west the gymnasium.

Colour was important. During construction the architects saw a potential problem with the long passages and called in artist Erich Wiesner. By painting the doors and panels in bright colours he eliminated the unwanted effect. Behnisch commented generously: "We found, not for the first time, that while introducing 'outsiders' is somewhat disturbing, they also enrich our work, forcing us out of our rut."

Südansicht von der Austraße / South view from Austrasse

Klassenring mit gläsernem Treppenhaus / Ring of classrooms with glass staircase

Lageplan
Site plan

Pausenhof
Schoolyard

Frei geformtes Treppenhaus am Raumring
Free-form staircase along the ring

Schnitt
Section

Grundriß Obergeschoß
Upper floor plan

Grundriß Erdgeschoß
Ground floor plan

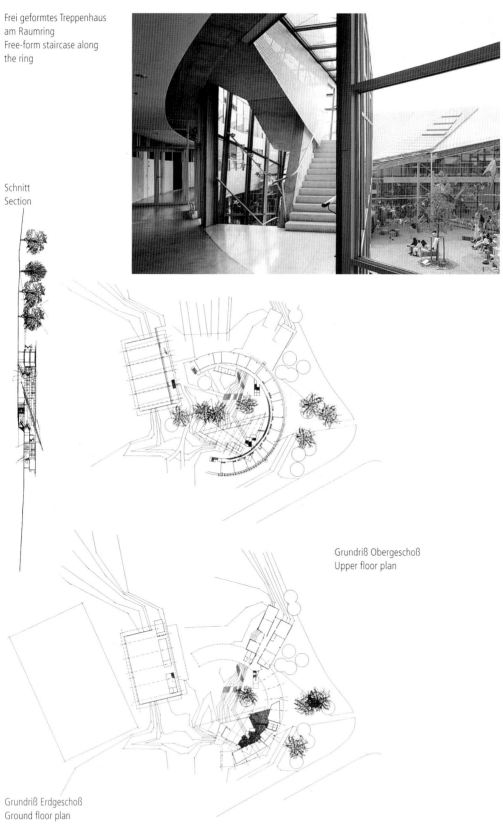

Treppenskulptur im Luftraum der Halle
Staircase sculpture in the hall's open space

Einweihungsfeier in der Halle
Opening celebration in the hall

St. Benno-Gymnasium
Dresden, 1996

Diese alte katholische, für ihre Musik berühmte Chorschule wurde von den Nationalsozialisten geschlossen und fiel dem Bombenkrieg zum Opfer. Nach der Wende 1989 wurde die Schule wiedereröffnet. Das in einer modernen Vorstadt östlich vom Stadtzentrum gelegene Baugelände ist ein langes, schmales Nordsüdgrundstück. Im Osten mußte es von einer verkehrsreichen Straße abgeschirmt werden, was den Gedanken eines linearen Gebäudes mit einer weitgehend geschlossenen Außenwand anregte. Der Hauptzugang erfolgt von einem neu angelegten städtischen Platz im Süden, im Norden endet die Anlage mit einer großen Sporthalle. Die nach Westen orientierten Klassenräume sind gruppenweise in unterschiedlichen Winkeln angeordnet; in den dadurch entstandenen Zwischenräumen liegen die großen Gemeinschaftsräume: die Versammlungs- und Verkehrshalle sowie die Bibliothek. Die wechselnde Ausrichtung der Klassentrakte betont die Identität der Teile und ermöglicht es, daß der dahinterliegende horizontale Verkehrsbereich sich fortlaufend und vielfältig zugleich entwickelt. Die Länge von 140 m wirkt nirgendwo bedrückend, sondern ist als lebendige Folge von räumlichen Ereignissen ausgebildet. Die große Wand wird sporadisch durch Fenster, Treppen und auskragende Erker unterbrochen, ohne ihren großen Maßstab zu zerstören, der sich Vorbeifahrenden einprägt und im Kontrast steht zur aufgelösten Ansicht dahinter. Wie bei der Schule in Öhringen wurde mit Hilfe des Künstlers Erich Wiesner ein kräftiges Farbsystem entwickelt.

St Benno grammar school
Dresden, 1996

This old catholic choir-school, famous for its music, was repressed by the Nazis, bombed in the war, and revived after the fall of the Wall in 1989. Part of a modern suburb east of the city centre, the site is a long thin plot running north-south. Protection was needed against a busy road to east, which prompted the idea of building along a wall on a linear principle. Entry is from a newly constructed urban square to south, and the school ends with a large sports-hall to north. Batches of classrooms set at contrasting angles face west, the gaps between them containing the major social spaces: first the hall for assembly and circulation, second the library. The changing orientations of the blocks both articulate the identities of the parts, and allow the linear circulation space behind to develop in a continuously varied manner. The 140 m length never becomes oppressive, but is developed as a rich sequence of spatial incidents. The great wall is broken sporadically with windows, stairs and projecting bays, but not enough to destroy its large scale, which registers for those in passing cars and contrasts with the fragmented face behind. As with the school at Öhringen, a bold colour scheme was devised with the help of artist Erich Wiesner.

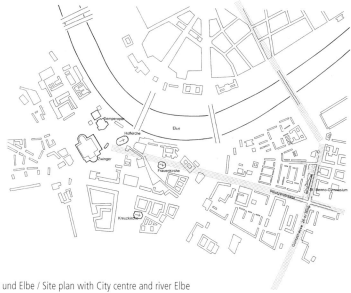

Lageplan mit Innenstadt und Elbe / Site plan with City centre and river Elbe

Halle
Hall

Klassenräume und Halle von
Süd-Westen
Classrooms and hall from the
south-west

Erschließungsflur und offene Treppenläufe
Circulation hallway and open stairs

Aufenthalts- und Flurbereich / Recreation and hallway area

Halle mit Verbindungstreppen / Hall with connecting stairs

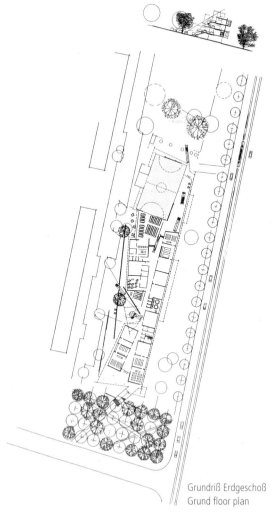

Schnitt
Section

Grundriß Erdgeschoß
Grund floor plan

Der blaue Rücken an der Güntzstraße / The "blue backside" on Güntzstrasse

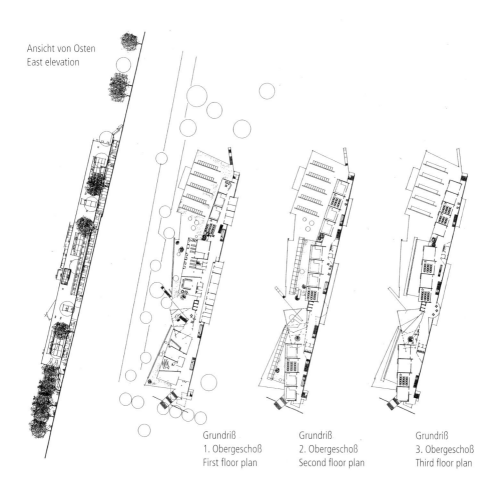

Ansicht von Osten
East elevation

Grundriß
1. Obergeschoß
First floor plan

Grundriß
2. Obergeschoß
Second floor plan

Grundriß
3. Obergeschoß
Third floor plan

Sportbauten

Sporthalle
Schwenningen, 1969

Dieser zeittypische Entwurf gehört zu einer Reihe vorfabrizierter Schulbauten, die Behnisch unter Verwendung von vorgefertigten Betonelementen (S. 30) plante, und ist Ausdruck einer sich streng wiederholenden Disziplin der Montage. Der gleichmäßig gerasterte, hier erstmalig als Stahlkonstruktion ausgeführte Baukörper verzichtet völlig auf einen Dachvorsprung und wird nur durch zweigeschossige Verglasung und ein auskragendes Schutzdach über dem Eingang aufgelockert. Im Innern bleibt das Tragwerk sichtbar, und die Oberlichter werden als in die flache Decke eingeschnittene Löcher behandelt. Dennoch zeigt die Organisation eine gewisse Raffinesse, indem der vorhandene Hang dazu genutzt wird, Eingänge auf verschiedenen Ebenen zu schaffen: für Sportler bzw. für Zuschauer. Das Publikum gelangt durch einen großen Vordereingang in einen doppelgeschoßhohen, verglasten Raum mit Garderoben und betritt die Halle über drei gerade Treppenläufe auf mittlerer Ebene. Von hier hat es Zugang zu den Galerieplätzen und zu den tiefergelegenen Sitzreihen, die zurückgeklappt werden können. Die Sportler kommen auf der Rückseite auf der oberen Ebene herein, betreten die Umkleiden über eine offene Galerie im Hallenraum, ziehen sich um und steigen dann hinab in die Arena. Unter den Umkleideräumen befinden sich Geräte- und Technikräume.

Buildings for Sport

School sports-hall
Schwenningen, 1969

Typical of its time, this design belongs to the series of prefabricated school buildings designed by Behnisch using precast concrete elements (p. 30), and expressing a hard repetitive discipline of assembly. The regular gridded box, here realised as a steel construction for the first time, with its roof edge completely suppressed, is relieved only by two-storey glazing and a projecting entrance canopy. Internally the structure is just visible and rooflights are treated as holes cut in a flat plane. The organisation has some subtlety, however, exploiting the given slope to provide contrasted entrances on opposite sides and at different levels, for athletes and spectators. The public get a grand front entrance into a double-height glazed space with cloakroom facilities, arriving at mid level in the hall via three straight staircases. From here they have access both to the gallery seating and to the lower banks of seats which can be folded away. Sports-people arrive at the back more informally at the upper level, change, then descend to the arena. The space under the changing rooms is given to equipment storage and plant rooms.

Perspektive des Innenraums / Perspective of interior space

Ansicht von Süden / View from the south

Schnitt
Section

Grundrisse Obergeschoß und Eingangsgeschoß

Upper floor and entrance floor plans

Turnhalle der Oskar-von-Miller-Realschule
Rothenburg ob der Tauber, 1970

Die Organisationsstruktur entspricht der von Schwenningen (S. 62), auch das orthogonale System der modularen Felder ist noch vorhanden; die Spannweite beträgt 12,5 m, die Breite 3 m. Aufgrund der Verwendung von Stahl und Glas liegen das Tragwerk und die Bauweise unvermutet offen. Das überstehende Dach und die transparenten Wände lassen den Bau pavillonähnlicher und weniger körperlich erscheinen. Das Erscheinungsbild wird durch Geländemodellierung und einen schützenden Vorbau erreicht. Die Turnhalle steht als wohlproportionierter, langer, niedriger Pavillon vor der berühmten mittelalterlichen Stadtmauer und fügt sich erstaunlich gut in den historischen Kontext ein. Das sichtbare Volumen der großen Halle wird verringert, da sie 1,5 m in den Boden versenkt ist. Weil das Terrain abfällt, liegt der Eingang an der Rückseite des Gebäudes 2,5 m über dem Hallenniveau. Auf dieser Ebene liegen die Umkleideräume, darunter Geräte- und Technikräume. Die offenen Umkleidekabinen stehen als separate Zellen im Zwischengeschoß; dadurch bleiben die Metalldecke und das Tragwerk durchgehend sichtbar. Große Träger durchdringen die Glaswand in einer Detailgestaltung, die fast zu einem Merkmal der Behnisch-Architektur geworden ist.

School sports-hall
Rothenburg on Tauber, 1970

The organisational strategy is similar to that at Schwenningen (p. 62), with the orthogonal discipline of structural bays still present, the span being 12.5 m and the bays 3 m. But suddenly structure and construction are laid bare through use of steel and glass. The projecting roof and transparent walls make the building more pavilion-like and less boxy, producing a contrast between the manipulation of the ground – earthworks – and the provision of a sheltering canopy. The sports-hall stands in front of the famous medieval town wall as a finely-proportioned long low pavilion, fitting its historical context remarkably well. The visual impact of the main hall is reduced by sinking it 1.5 m into the ground, and since the site slopes, the building is entered 2.5 m above hall level at the back. The entrance leads to changing rooms at the same level, with storage and plant below. Open changing cubicles stand as separate cells on the intermediate floor, leaving the metal ceiling deck and structure to run through uninterrupted. Main beams penetrate the glass wall with a detail that became almost a Behnisch cliché.

Die Sporthalle von Süd-Osten vor der Stadtsilhouette / Sports-hall from the south-east in front of skyline

Die Halle vom Spielfeld aus / Hall seen from the court

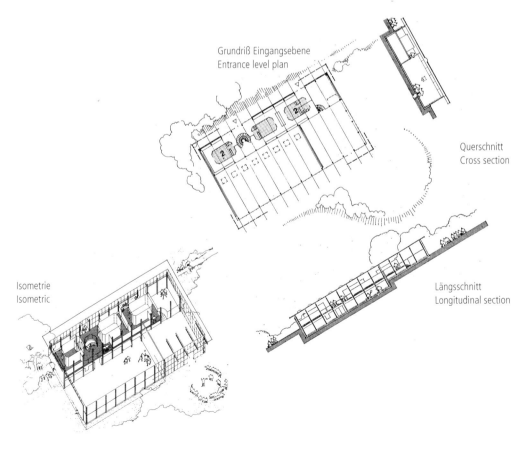

Grundriß Eingangsebene
Entrance level plan

Querschnitt
Cross section

Isometrie
Isometric

Längsschnitt
Longitudinal section

Olympiapark
München, 1972

Im Jahre 1967 gewann Behnisch den Wettbewerb für das Gesamtkonzept und die Hauptsportstätten der Olympischen Spiele 1972. Der südliche Teil des Geländes am Nordrand der Münchener City war Abladeplatz für Millionen Tonnen Trümmer aus kriegszerstörten Bauten. Die dadurch entstandenen künstlichen Hügel waren zwar mit traurigen Erinnerungen belastet, aber das Material war, ebenso wie das natürliche Kiesbett darunter, formbar und ließ sich zu einer neuen Landschaft aus Hügeln und Seen umgestalten – eine von Anfang an verfolgte und mit Hilfe eines Sandmodells entwickelte Leitidee, die axiale Auslegungen ausschloß. Ein vorhandener Kanal wurde zum zentralen See aufgestaut, die verbleibenden Schuttmassen wurden zu einem schönen, der City zugewandten Hügel geformt. Die großen Arenen sind locker zwischen See und Stadtautobahn plaziert, die Tribünen wie antike Theater in die Hänge eingefügt, so daß geschlossene Bauten nicht entstehen konnten. Jede einzelne Anlage wurde zu einer scheinbar natürlichen Bodenlandschaft mit einer zeltähnlichen Dachlandschaft. Die Landschaftsgestaltung in Zusammenarbeit mit dem Landschaftsarchitekten Günther Grzimek erforderte großes Geschick, weil außer den Sitzreihen auch alle übrigen Nebeneinrichtungen mit den zugehörigen unterirdischen Erschließungsstraßen untergebracht werden mußten. Das verursachte beträchtliche Probleme. Zum Beispiel drohte die Forderung nach vorschriftsmäßig dimensionierten Fluchtwegen eine künftige Nutzung als Park zu erschweren; es wurden jedoch Möglichkeiten gefunden, die Besucherströme freier durch das Gelände zu führen.

Die Seilnetzdächer werden häufig Frei Otto zugeschrieben, dessen Beitrag sicher von großer Bedeutung war, aber nicht als eigentlicher Urheber des Projekts. Seine Bauten in Montreal waren die entscheidenden Vorgänger; das Dach des Münchener Wettbewerbsentwurfs wurde von Behnisch & Partnern zusammen mit dem Ingenieur Heinz Isler geplant. Sie schlugen ein durchgehendes, von Masten und Seilen getragenes Zelt vor, das sich vom Hauptstadion über zwei weitere Hallen erstreckte, mit einer Abzweigung zur Überdachung der Erschließungsbrücke über die Stadtautobahn. Es war größer als alle bisher ausgeführten Seilnetzdächer, und es gab Zweifel, ob das machbar wäre. Mit der Weiterentwicklung wurden die führenden Ingenieure Leonhardt + Andrä unter der Leitung von Jörg Schlaich beauftragt. Frei Otto wurde als Berater hinzugezogen, und schließlich wurde das Seilnetzdach in modifizierter Weise realisiert, das heißt in veränderter Form und mit anderer Stützenstellung, aber Behnischs ursprünglichen Intentionen ent-

Olympic Park
Munich, 1972

A competition was held in 1967 for the games of 1972, won by Behnisch for the general concept. The south part of the site on the northern outskirts of the city was the dumping ground for millions of tons of rubble from wartime destruction. The artificial hills so created carried an important memory, but the material was mouldable, as was the natural gravel beneath it, and so could be adjusted to create a new landscape of hills and lakes. From the start this was the key idea, developed with the help of a sandmodel. Axial layouts were avoided. An existing stream was dammed for the central lake, and the remaining mass of debris shaped into a hill on the side facing the city. The large arenas were freely placed between lake and motorway, their raked seating absorbed into the hillsides like classical theatres, precluding the need for box-like structures. Each arena became a seemingly natural groundscape with a tent-like skyscape. The landscape design in collaboration with landscape architect Günther Grzimek involved great sleight of hand, for along with the ranks of seating most of the other subordinate facilities had to be absorbed, along with servicing provision via underground roads. There were considerable problems: the emergency escape requirements threatened to impose paths at a scale quite out of proportion for final use as a park, for example, but ways were found of accommodating the flows without making this requirement too obvious.

The cable net roofs are often attributed to Frei Otto whose contribution was certainly important, but he did not originate the design. His work at Montreal was the crucial precedent, but the roof of the Munich competition project was designed by Behnisch & Partners with Heinz Isler as engineer. They proposed a continuous tent supported by masts and cables which would spread from the main arena over the two other halls, with even a branch covering the entrance bridge across the autobahn. It was larger than any cable-net roof yet built, and there were doubts whether it could be done. To develop it further the leading engineers Leonhardt + Andrä were commissioned, with Jörg Schlaich as project leader. Frei Otto was brought in as adviser, and eventually the cable-net roof went ahead in a modified form: that is to a different shape and modified mast-positions, but following Behnisch's original intention. New technologies were developed and engineering stretched to the limit. Significant relationships with firms and technologists were set up, for new components had to be invented. Large scale steel casting was reintroduced for the cable anchors, for example.

sprechend. Neue Techniken wurden entwickelt und Ingenieurbauweisen bis an die Grenze des Möglichen geführt. Wichtige Verbindungen mit Firmen und Technologen entstanden, denn es mußten neue Elemente erfunden werden. Zum Beispiel wurden großmaßstäbliche Stahlgußteile für Seilverankerungen und Umlenkpunkte entwickelt.

Wettbewerbsentwurf 1967.
Lageplan der Gesamtanlage
Competition design 1967.
General site plan

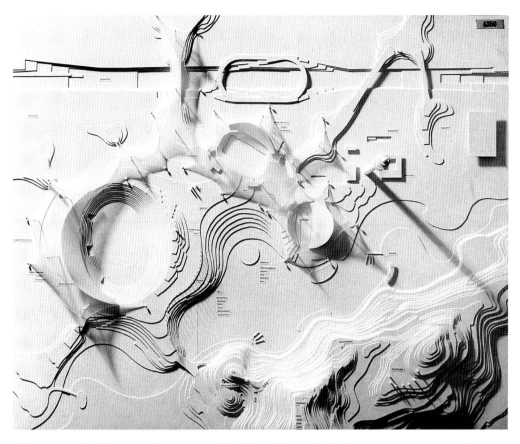
Wettbewerbsmodell mit Olympischen Zentrum, See und Berg / Competition model with Olympic centre, lake and mountain

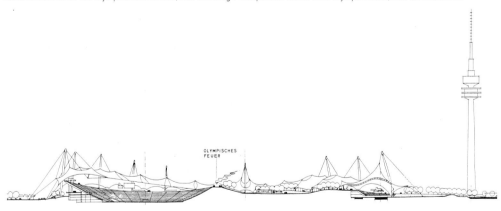
West-Ost-Schnitt, Ausführungsstand / West-east section as realized

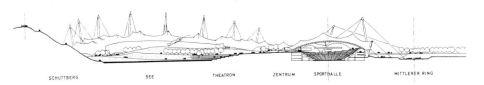
Nord-Süd-Schnitt / North-south section

Das Olympiastadion vom Berg / Olympic stadium seen from the mountain

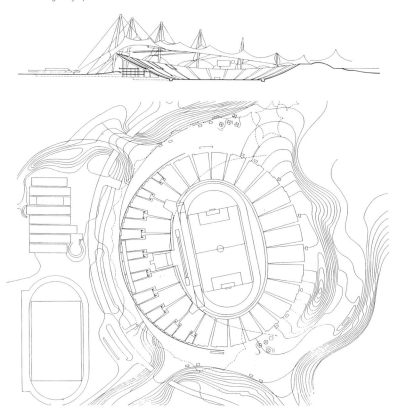

Stadion. Schnitt und Schüsselaufsicht / Stadium. Section and plan

Sporthalle und Schwimmhalle vom Berg während der Olympischen Spiele
Sports-hall and swimming hall from the mountain during the Olympic games

Luftaufnahme von Süden. Olympischer Zustand / Aerial view from the south. State during the Olympic games

Zuschauer im Stadion und auf dem Berg / Spectators in the stadium and on the mountain

Der zentrale Sportstättenbereich während einer Aufführung der Rolling Stones
Central sports area during a performance by the Rolling Stones

Westtribüne des Olympiastadions
West stands of Olympic Stadium

Sporthalle, heute Olympiahalle
Sports-hall, today Olympic Hall

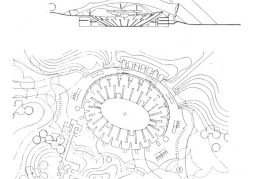

Sporthalle. Schnitt und Grundriß Foyerebene
Sports-hall. Section and plan of foyer level

Inneres der Schwimmhalle / Interior of swimming hall

Wintersport auf dem Berg
Winter sports on mountain

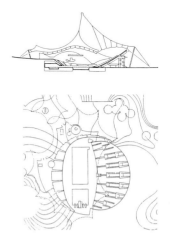

Parklandschaft
Landscape of park

Schwimmhalle mit temporärer Tribüne
Schnitt und Grundriß Foyerebene
Swimming hall with temporary stands
Section and foyer level plan

Schwimmhalle mit Fernsehturm, See und Wasserwolke von Heinz Mack
Swimming hall with TV tower, lake and Heinz Mack's water cloud

Trainings- und Aufwärmhalle für die Olympiade
München, 1972

Diese Halle ist Teil der Olympia-Anlage. Ihr Dach mit einer freien Spannweite von 90 × 45 m überdeckt eine 200 m-Laufbahn mit halbkreisförmigen Kurven. Die Arena ist tiefer gelegt, ebenso wie die auf einer Seite angefügten Umkleide- und Serviceräume. Die Halle folgt dem gleichen System wie die Hauptbauten. Das Dach mit einer Weite von 52 m ist in 12,5 m große Felder unterteilt, die auf Fachwerkträgern mit dreieckigem Querschnitt aufliegen, welche wiederum auf beiden Seiten von stählernen Stützenpaaren getragen werden. Über jedem Träger verläuft ein Oberlichtband, dazwischen schwingen sich tieferliegende Flächen auf Sekundärträgern. Der orthogonale Umriß des Daches wird von der Konstruktion bestimmt; über bestimmten Dachfeldern ist die Dachdecke jedoch vorgezogen, um einen Schutz zu bieten. Zwischen diese aufgelöste Dachkonstruktion und das Terrain ist eine Glaswand gestellt, die den Krümmungen der Laufbahn auf beiden Seiten des Gebäudes folgt und einen Gegenpol zum rechtwinkligen System der Konstruktion bildet. Die großen Träger durchdringen auf spektakuläre Weise die Glaswand.

Training and warm-up hall for Munich Olympics
1972

This hall is part of the Olympic complex, containing a semicircular-ended running track with a clear span of 90 × 45 m. With running track carved out of the ground and changing and service rooms buried on one side, the hall follows the same pattern as the main Olympic buildings in a more modest way. The 52 m span roof is divided into bays of 12.5 m carried on huge trusses of triangular section supported on each side by paired steel posts. Over each truss is a rooflight, and a series of valley roofs on secondary trusses are slung between. The structure dictates its own rectangular plan shape, but over certain bays the intermediate roof is extended to provide a canopy. Between this disciplined roof and the groundworks is a skin of glass, which follows the curved running track around the ends of the building, playing against the rectangular system. The great trusses penetrate the glass wall in a dramatic manner.

Die Aufwärmhalle vom Stadionumgang
Warm-up hall seen from stadium gallery

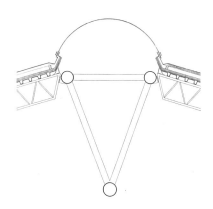

Dreigurtbinder. Schnitt
Triangular lattice beam. Section

Ostseite. Detail mit aufgeständertem Dreigurtbinder
East side. Detail of supported triangular lattice beam

Innenraum in Längsrichtung / Interior in longitudinal direction

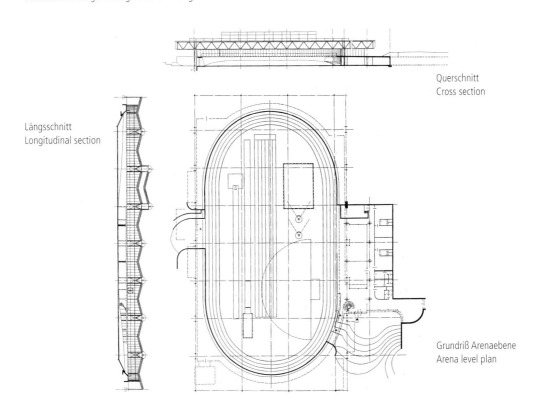

Querschnitt
Cross section

Längsschnitt
Longitudinal section

Grundriß Arenaebene
Arena level plan

Schulsporthalle
Lorch, 1976

Die Turnhalle in Rothenburg (S. 63) mit einer Spannweite von nur 12,5 m war mit einfachen Walzstahlträgern ausgeführt worden. Die Dachkonstruktionen der nachfolgenden Schulsporthallen sind komplexer und differenzierter, teils um größere Spannweiten zu erzielen, teils um eine kleinmaßstäblichere Behandlung der Außenfronten zu erreichen. Lorch hat zwei ineinandergreifende Tragsysteme, die eine Spannweite von fast 30 m ermöglichen. Die innere Weite beträgt 20 m unter einem Flachdach, getragen von einer Reihe von unterspannten Stahlträgern. Im Abstand von 3 m leiten sie ihre Lasten über ein Randprofil auf eine Reihe von Y- und T-förmigen Tragelementen im Abstand von 6 m ab, die im Außenbereich rückverankert sind. Der gestalterische Vorteil besteht darin, daß durch geneigte Dächer das sichtbare Volumen der Halle reduziert werden kann und maßstäblich niedrigere Eingangsbereiche entstehen. Foyer und Treppen sind hier nicht wie in früheren Hallen unter einem Dach zusammengefaßt, sondern die Treppen als Anbauten behandelt und von einer offenen Glashaut umschlossen. Die unterschiedliche Behandlung der Außenseiten ermöglicht auch eine klarere Unterscheidung zwischen Tal- und Hangseite. Die nach allen Seiten geneigten Metalldächer erzeugen ein geschlossenes, scheunenähnliches Erscheinungsbild, anders als bei früheren Hallen. Die aufgrund der geneigten Dächer reduzierten Fassadenflächen verstärken die Wirkung des Lichteinfalls durch die zentralen Oberlichter.

School sports-hall
Lorch, 1976

With a span of only 12.5 m, the roof at Rothenburg (p. 63) was carried on simple rolled steel joists. The roof structures on subsequent school sports-halls are more complex and differentiated, partly to produce larger clear spans and partly to allow smaller scale treatment of the building edges. Lorch has two interacting structural systems giving a clear span of nearly 30 m. The central 20 m span supporting a flat roof is carried on a series of trusses made by adding downstand tension elements to steel joists. These occur at 3 m centres, transmitting their load via a frame to a series of Y- and T-shaped steel portals at 6 m centres, tensioned along the outer edge. The architectural advantage is that it brings the roof down at the outside, giving a gentler profile and smaller scale at the point of entry. Rather than being subsumed under the pavilion roof as in earlier halls, foyer and stairs are treated as additions, set under their own subsidiary roof formed by the portal element, but setting up a free glass envelope to run within and beyond it following circulation requirements. Specialisation of the perimeter also allows clearer differentiation between front and back. To sides and rear sloping metal roofs produce a closed, barn-like image in contrast with the lightness of earlier halls. After environmental problems with earlier designs, sidelight was restricted by sloping roofs while toplight increased from linear skylights running across the main structure.

Lageplan Progymnasium und Sporthalle / Site plan of grammar school and sports-hall

Das Halleninnere mit Mobiltribüne / Hall interior with movable stands

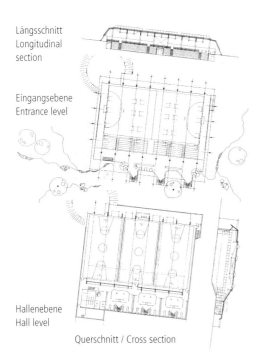

Längsschnitt
Longitudinal section

Eingangsebene
Entrance level

Hallenebene
Hall level

Querschnitt / Cross section

Rückverankerung des Dachtragwerks auf der Nordseite
Anchoring of roof structure on the north side

Ansicht von Süden / View from the south

Sporthalle
Sindelfingen, 1977

Diese Halle ist von ähnlicher Größe und folgt im Ansatz den gleichen Prinzipien wie die Münchener Aufwärmhalle (S. 74), ist aber differenzierter. Es handelt sich um eine öffentliche Arena mit mehreren Tausend Besucherplätzen, einem Foyer und wesentlich größerem Volumen. Sie ist in den Boden versenkt, ebenso wie die Nebenräume und eine Anlage mit acht Bowlingbahnen. Das Stahldach hat eine Spannweite von 54 m. Im Abstand von 13 m liegen dreieckförmige Fachwerkbinder mit der Spitze nach oben. Die Zwischenflächen sind nahezu flach gedeckt, die seitlichen Binderflächen verglast und bilden Lichtbänder in den Decken. Dadurch entsteht eine gegliederte Decke mit erstaunlich gleichmäßiger Lichtqualität. Außen verleiht die lebendige Folge der Lichtraupen dem Gebäude eine einprägsame Identität und offenbart seinen Maßstab. Die Enden der Binder sind unterschiedlich ausgebildet. Im Westen wurden sie abgeknickt und bis zum Boden heruntergeführt. Die Zuschauer sitzen dort wie unter einem Mansarddach. Im Osten schließen das Foyer und der Eingangsbereich an die Arena an. Deshalb stehen die Binder dort auf Stahlstützen, und an das Hauptdach ist eine leichtere, niedrigere Konstruktion angefügt. Der Grundrißform folgend, wurden an den Schmalseiten der Halle ähnliche Dachkonstruktionen verwendet – eine Variante des sekundären Tragsystems zwischen den Bindern. Dadurch war es möglich, das Dach auf allen Seiten sanft abzusenken, die Zugänge kleinmaßstäblicher zu gestalten und die Masse des Gebäudes in der Landschaft zu reduzieren.

Sports-hall
Sindelfingen, 1977

This hall is of similar size and follows the same initial principles as the Munich training hall (p. 74), but is more subtle. It is a public arena requiring large numbers of seats, a foyer, and a taller space. The arena is carved out of the ground. Services, ancillary rooms and even a bowling alley are also buried. The steel roof has triangular trusses spanning 54 m with bays of 13 m, the trusses inverted to project upward into rooflights, while intermediate roofs are flat. This produces a gentle ceiling with a surprisingly even quality of light. On the outside a dramatic sequence of fin-like elements give the building a recognisable identity and reveal its scale. The truss ends are treated asymmetrically in sympathy with the programme. To west, banks of spectator seating must be contained with no outlook, so the west ends of the trusses are cranked over to meet the ground, the roof being carried into a mansard-like side wall. To east the arena adjoins foyer and entrance, so the trusses are carried on steel posts and the main roof gives way to a lower, lighter structure for entrance and foyer. In recognition of the plan shape the end trusses are shorter, and the curves of spectator seating covered by a low roof, a variant of the secondary structural system between the trusses. This brings the roof down gently, assuring that the approaches to the building are scaled down, and that its impact on the landscape is reduced.

Isometrie
Isometric

Fußpunkt der Dachraupen auf der Westseite
Anchor point of roof elements on the west side

Ansicht von Südwesten / View from the south-west

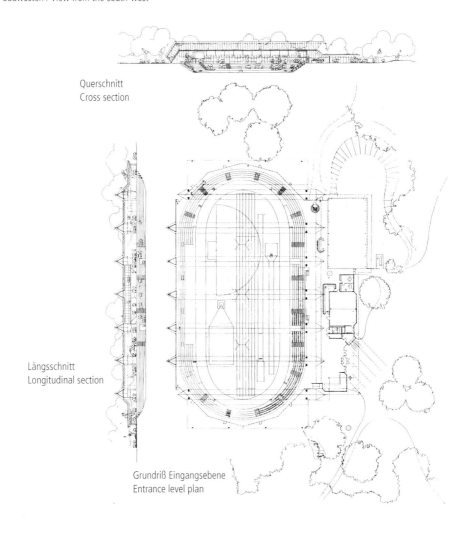

Querschnitt
Cross section

Längsschnitt
Longitudinal section

Grundriß Eingangsebene
Entrance level plan

Das Halleninnere von der Arenaebene / Hall interior seen from the arena level

Foyer mit Regiekanzel
Foyer with control platform

Südkurve
South curve

Westseite der Zuschauertribüne / West side of stands

Sporthalle
Sulzbach an der Murr, 1984

Wie die anderen späten Schulsporthallen ist auch diese Halle als Pavillon behandelt, aber ergänzt durch einen niedrigeren Anbau für den Eingang und die Umkleiden. Sowohl das konstruktive System als auch die Hierarchie der Organisation sind klarer geworden. Es gibt drei statische Bereiche: Die entscheidende Spannweite wird durch 20 m lange Binder erreicht, die Felder von 5 m Breite bilden. Querbinder liegen über der Deckenebene und bilden jeweils ein verglastes Oberlicht. Die zu überspannende Länge von 23 m wird reduziert auf 20 m durch T-förmige Tragelemente wie in Lorch (S. 76), auf denen diese Binder aufliegen. Außerhalb der Glashülle sind diese Elemente nach unten rückverankert. Dieser zweite statische Bereich unterteilt den Innenraum nicht, denn die horizontale Decke läuft ununterbrochen durch. Die Zusatzkonstruktion ermöglicht die Ausbildung eines ganz dünnen Dachrands, dem die Sporthalle ihr pavillonähnliches Erscheinungsbild verdankt. Der weite Dachvorsprung reduziert die Sonneneinstrahlung. Innenliegende Jalousien halten die niedrigstehende Wintersonne ab. Auf der anderen Seite liegt jeder Binder auf einer Pendelstütze auf. Dahinter liegt der dritte statische Bereich, ein unabhängiges niedrigeres und kleinmaßstäblicheres System von Trägern, die entlang der Rückwand und dem überdachten Eingang, dem Foyer und den Umkleiden an der Erschließungsseite laufen. Dieser Bereich ist zur Betonung des übereck angeordneten Eingangs abgeschrägt. Die Dachsparren sind aus Holz, auch die zwischen den Hauptbindern, während weiß gestrichene Stahlbinder die größeren Lasten aufnehmen. Das verstärkt die Ablesbarkeit der statischen Hierarchie. Die horizontale Schichtung der Dachkonstruktion geht bis zur sichtbar belassenen Dachfläche aus Holzbohlen.

School sports-hall
Sulzbach on Murr, 1984

As in other late school sports-halls, the main body of the building is treated as a pavilion, but combined with a lower addition for entry and changing. Both structural order and hierarchy of organisation become clearer. There are three structural zones, the basic span being achieved by 20 m trusses forming 5 m bays. The truss depth is kept above ceiling level by incorporating each within a projecting glazed skylight. The clear span is extended to 23 m by carrying the trusses at one end on a series of T-shaped portal elements as at Lorch (p. 76), again tensioned along the outer edge beyond the glass envelope. This second structural zone does not divide the internal space, for the horizontal ceiling runs through uninterrupted. The portal structure carries the flat roof out to a delicate thin edge, presenting a pavilion-like appearance to the sports field. The deep roof overhang and spectator gallery limit solar penetration to a low angle, while internal roller blinds limit the low winter sun. At the rear each truss is taken vertically by a column, and beyond this is the third structural zone, an independent lower and smaller-scale system of trusses which runs along the back and the approach side covering entry, foyer and changing arrangements. It skews in celebration of the corner entrance. Smaller roof spans are timber, even between the main trusses, while white-painted steel elements take the larger loads. This intensifies the reading of structural hierarchy. The visible layering of construction goes as far as the exposed plywood roof deck.

Die Halle in Querrichtung / Cross view of hall

Isometrie
Isometric

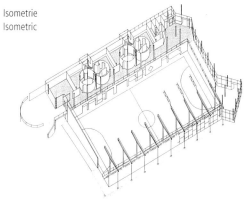

Ansicht von Süden / View from the south

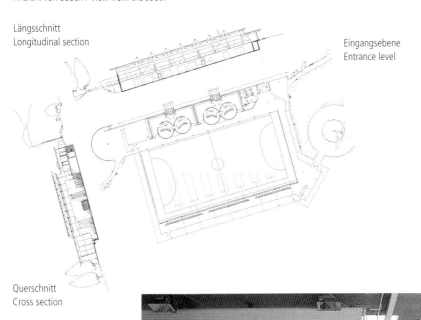

Längsschnitt
Longitudinal section

Eingangsebene
Entrance level

Querschnitt
Cross section

Das Dachtragwerk in Längs-richtung
Roof structure in longitudinal direction

Sozialbauten

Alten- und Pflegeheim
Reutlingen, 1977

Ein bestehendes Altenheim aus dem Jahre 1920 sollte im Innenbereich eines von Einfamilienhäusern umgebenen Vorstadtblocks erweitert werden. Durch schräge Plazierung eines S-förmigen Baukörpers auf dem Grundstück optimierten die Architekten die Orientierung und teilten die Anlage in überschaubare Einheiten für das Alten- und das Pflegeheim auf. Beide dreieckigen Elemente, aus denen der S-förmige Plan besteht, konzentrieren sich auf eine zentrale, von oben belichtete Halle mit Aufzügen und Treppen. Die schmale «Taille» zwischen den Trakten der Anlage ermöglicht seitliche Ausblicke. Ein Großteil der Räume wird von dieser Halle erschlossen und liegt nicht an langen, düsteren Korridoren. Im Osten schließt der neue Komplex mit einem verglasten Bauglied an das alte Gebäude; der neue Haupteingang ist in einen freistehenden, sechseckigen Glaspavillon gesetzt. Beim Eintritt trifft man zuerst auf den Eßbereich und die Aufenthaltsräume, die auch Besuchern und den Bewohnern des alten Gebäudes zugänglich sind. Die oberen Ebenen mit den auf Stützen gestellten Privaträumen laufen in diesem Teil des Gebäudes durch und lassen das Erdgeschoß bis zum zentralen Lichthof offen. An der Nordseite der Anlage befindet sich die Anlieferung, während die Süd- und Westseite zu großzügig gestalteten Gärten orientiert sind. Die Schrägstellung der Räume ermöglicht die Anordnung von Bädern und Eingangsnischen an der Innenseite, während ein erstaunlich komplexes Arrangement aus Erker, Balkon und geschütztem Freisitz sich an der Außenseite entfaltet. Schindeln aus Red Cedar als Wandverkleidung und ein flach geneigtes Welleternitdach tragen zu einem freundlichen Erscheinungsbild dieses großen und durchweg modernen Gebäudes bei.

Social Buildings

Old people's home and nursing home
Reutlingen, 1977

An existing old people's home built in the 1920s was to be extended on the inner land of a suburban block surrounded by private houses. Through placing an S-shaped figure obliquely on the site, the architects both optimised the orientation and subdivided the accommodation into manageable units. Each of the two triangular figures making up the S-plan focuses on a central toplit hall with lifts, stairs and a vertical well, while the narrow 'waist' of the building between them allows views to the sides. A large number of rooms was accommodated without the curse of long, dingy corridors. To east, the new complex connects to the older building with a glazed link, the new mainentrance set in a free-standing hexagonal glass pavilion. The first rooms encountered on entry are the dining area and sitting rooms, shared with visitors and inhabitants of the old building. Upper ranks of private rooms carry through on columns in this part of the building, leaving the ground floor open as far as the central well. The north side of the complex allows service access, while south and west look into lavishly landscaped gardens. Skewed placing of rooms allows bathrooms and entry niches to be accommodated on the inside, while a surprisingly complex arrangement of bay, balcony and sheltered external sitting area develops at the outside. Natural shingles and a shallow pitched roof soften the external image of this large and thoroughly modern construction.

Altenheimzimmer
Room in old people's home

Pflegeheimzimmer
Room in nursing home

Altenheim und Pflegeheim, Gartenseite / Old people's home and nursing home, garden side

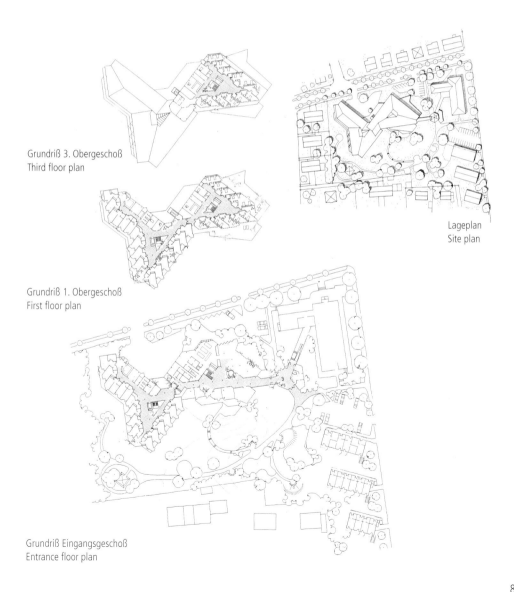

Grundriß 3. Obergeschoß
Third floor plan

Grundriß 1. Obergeschoß
First floor plan

Lageplan
Site plan

Grundriß Eingangsgeschoß
Entrance floor plan

Erker mit Loggien
Bay window with loggias

Laube
Arbour

Wintergarten
Winter garden

Pforte mit Pflegeheim, im Hintergrund Georgenberg
Gate with nursing home, Georgenberg behind

Altenheim. Gebäudeecke im Süden
Old people's home. Southern corner of building

Pforte
Gate

Kindergarten
Stuttgart-Neugereut, 1977

Von außen gesehen, ist dieses eingeschossige, zu Füßen hoher Wohnbebauung plazierte Gebäude eines der weniger spektakulären Bauwerke von Behnisch. Im Innern zeigt sich jedoch ein anderes Bild. Die Einzelheiten entsprechen dort der Welt der Kinder und ihrer Phantasie. Seine geschlossene, nach Nordwesten gerichtete Seite enthält die Nebenräume. Nach Südosten öffnen sich die Gruppenräume mit Glaswänden zu teilweise überdeckten Terrassen und zum Garten. Die Grundrißorganisation ist relativ einfach: je zwei Gruppenräume, getrennt durch eine gemeinsam genutzte Halle; aber die Form der Anlage erzeugt eine lange Außenwand mit Nischen, welche die Kinder auf unterschiedliche Weise einnehmen und interpretieren können – als Haus, Schiff oder Höhle. Es entsteht auch eine Vielfalt von Schwellenbereichen zwischen inneren und äußeren Spielräumen. Natürliche Materialien herrschen vor, vorwiegend unbehandeltes Holz mit seiner warmen Oberfläche. Die Bodenflächen sind ebenfalls liebevoll in unterschiedlicher Textur gestaltet. Das Gebäude entspricht der Vorstellung, daß kleine Kinder sich eher dort zu Hause fühlen, wo sie etwas berühren und spüren können, als in Räumen und Formen, die sich an der Erwachsenenwelt orientieren.

Kindergarten
Stuttgart-Neugereut, 1977

Seen from without, this single-storey building tucked into the corner of a large housing estate is the least spectacular of Behnisch works, but its generous small-scale inner world is dedicated to the imagination of the child. The blind back wall to north-west carries wet services, while the building opens to south-east with glass walls and partly covered terraces giving onto a small garden. Plan organisation is relatively simple, with two pairs of group rooms divided by a shared hall, but the complex shape generates a long perimeter with corners to be inhabited and imagined in different ways – a house, a ship, a cave? It also produces a diversity of threshold conditions between rooms and outside play areas. Natural materials dominate, mainly naked timber with its warm surfaces, forming tiny windows and other idiosyncratic details. Ground surfaces are also elaborated and varied in texture. The building responds to the idea that small children are more at home with what they can touch and feel than with space and form seen at a distance.

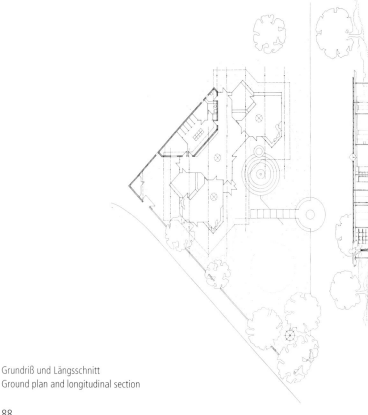

Grundriß und Längsschnitt
Ground plan and longitudinal section

Aufenthaltsraum
Group room

Übergang vom Gebäude zum Garten mit Clematis
Transition between building and garden with climbing plants

Überdachter Freibereich / Covered outside area

Kindergarten
Stuttgart-Luginsland, 1990

Dieser Bau mit seinem unkonventionellen Erscheinungsbild ist eines der widersprüchlichsten Projekte von Behnisch, obgleich er von seinen jungen Nutzern und deren Betreuerinnen im allgemeinen geschätzt wird. Er vertritt auch ein völlig anderes architektonisches Image als sein früher entstandenes Pendant in Neugereut (S. 88). An das Ende einer Vorstadtstraße gesetzt, mit Weinbergen als Hintergrund, handelt es sich unverkennbar um ein gestrandetes Schiff. Diese von Behnisch persönlich eingebrachte Idee stammt von einem erfolglosen früheren Versuch, die Überreste eines wirklichen Schiffes in einen Kindergarten einzubeziehen; hier wurde es jedoch künstlich geschaffen. Die beiden Geschosse sind für verschiedene Gruppen bestimmt; die obere Ebene wird über einen Steg an der Nordseite betreten. Im nach Osten orientierten Bug liegen die Sozialräume, im am Boden verankerten Heck die Nebenräume. Die schrägen Wände bilden ungewöhnliche Bereiche, die das Wahrnehmungsvermögen herausfordern, wie die angelsächsische Rummelplatzattraktion «The crooked house». Der Bau spiegelt die von Phantasie erfüllte Offenheit und Ungebundenheit der Kindheit, und seine spielerische Form verrät den Zweck. Die schwierige Frage war, wie buchstäblich schiffsgleich man den Bau gestalten sollte, denn es mußte Raum für die eigene phantasiereiche Interpretation des Kindes verbleiben. Glücklicherweise ist der ungewöhnliche Charakter des Gebäudes nicht nur für das Äußere prägend, sondern setzt sich im Innern fort.

Kindergarten
Stuttgart-Luginsland, 1990

With its unconventional image this has been one of the Behnisch office's most controversial projects, though it is generally liked by its child users and their carers. It also assumes an architectural role very different from that of its its earlier cousin at Neugereut (p. 88). Set at the end of a suburban street with vineyards as a backdrop, it is unmistakeably a stranded ship. Promoted by Behnisch personally, this idea was derived from an unsuccessful earlier attempt to incorporate the remains of a real ship in a kindergarten, but this time it was artificially created. The two floors are for different groups, the upper entered via a gang-plank on the northern side. Social rooms take the open east-facing prow, services the grounded stern. The leaning walls create unorthodox rooms which challenge perception, like the fairground attraction 'the crooked house'. The building reflects well the imaginative open-ness and lawlessness of childhood, and its playful form reveals its purpose. The difficult question was how literally ship-like to make it, for there must be room for the child's own imaginative interpretation. Fortunately the unusual character is not just a facade image, but continues within.

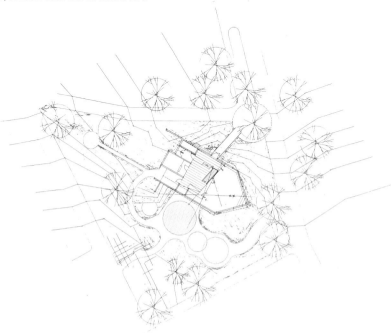

Lageplan
Site plan

Ansicht von Süd-Westen / View from the south-west

Nord-Ost-Seite, mit Grabkapelle auf dem Württemberg
Noth-east side, with burial chapel on the Württemberg

Grundriß Eingangsebene
Entrance level plan

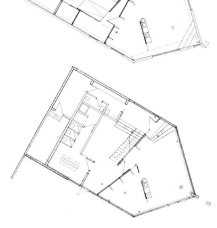

Grundriß Hanggeschoß
Lower level plan

Halle Eingangsebene / Entrance level hall

Giebelseite im Nord-Westen
North-west gable front

Die Kinder als Matrosen
The children as sailors

Bug
Bow

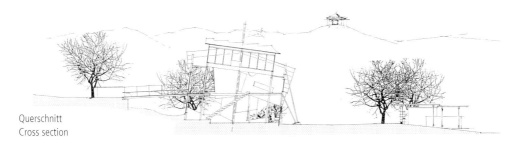
Querschnitt
Cross section

Oberer Aufenthaltsraum
Upper group room

Sozialer Wohnungsbau
Ingolstadt-Hollerstauden, 1997

Social housing
Ingolstadt-Hollerstauden, 1997

Angesichts seines langjährigen Engagements für soziales Bauen ist das Fehlen von Wohnungsbau in Behnischs bisherigem Werk bis zum Ende der neunziger Jahre verwunderlich. Hier handelt es sich um die erste Stufe einer großen Bebauung in einem neu entstehenden Vorort von Ingolstadt für eine katholische Wohlfahrtsorganisation. Sie sollte ursprünglich 70 Altenwohnungen, 30 Familien-Reihenhäuser und 60 Wohneinheiten für Studenten umfassen. Geplant wurden sie als zwei- und dreigeschossige horizontale, nord-süd- bzw. ost-west-orientierte, locker zu Innenhöfen und Fußgängerwegen angeordnete Riegel. Gebaut wurden zunächst 37 Wohnungen. Aufgrund des geringen Etats mußten sie klein und einfach geschnitten, die Materialien preisgünstig und die Details schlicht sein. Da Zuschnitt und Größe der Wohnungen durch die Förderrichtlinien weitgehend unveränderbar waren, wandte sich die Aufmerksamkeit der Architekten zwangsläufig der Fassadengliederung zu. Auf der Eingangsseite wurden die Fahrstühle, Treppenhäuser und Laubengänge zusammengefaßt und mit Glasdächern versehen. Auf der anderen, individuelleren Seite, die kleinen Gärten und Grünflächen zugewandt ist, wurden Vor- und Rücksprünge als Balkone oder Erker ausgebildet, wiederum unter dem Schutz eines Glasdachs. Weitere Vielfalt wurde durch besondere Behandlung der Blockendseiten erzielt sowie durch Variieren der Verkleidung: von Holzplanken bis zu Verputz in frischen Farben. Diese Variationen reduzieren den Maßstab, verbergen die Monotonie der Grundkonzeption und erzeugen eine menschliche Atmosphäre. Die Siedlung wirkt kostspieliger, als sie war.

With their long-standing commitment to social building, the lack of housing in Behnisch's oeuvre prior to the late 1990s is surprising. This is the first phase of a large development in a poor suburb of Ingolstadt for a catholic welfare organisation. Altogether it will include 70 pensioner flats, 30 terraced houses for families, and 60 student flats. They are planned as a series of two or three-storey linear blocks running north-south or east-west, and juxtaposed to form loose courts and pedestrian alleyways. Parking is restricted to the northern and eastern edges. 37 apartments were built in the first phase. Because of the low budget, the flats had to be small and boxy, the materials cheap and details simple. Most architectural effort went into the articulation of the facades. On the approach side this was a matter of elaborating the applied layer of lifts, stairs and galleries with glass roofs. On the other, more private side projections and recesses were formed as balconies or bays, again under the shelter of an added glass roof. Further liveliness was achieved by special treatment to block ends and by varying the cladding from timber boarding to brightly painted render. These variations bring the scale down, conceal the mechanistic nature of the basic construction and create a humane atmosphere. It looks more expensive than it was.

Modellaufsicht der Gesamtanlage
View of site model

Südost-Ansicht der südorientierten Reihenhäuser / South-east view of row houses facing south

1. Bauabschnitt mit 37 Seniorenwohnungen, Ansicht von Osten   First building phase with 37 pensioner flats, view from the east

Erschließungsseite der Ost-West orientierten Wohnungen / Access side of the flats organised in east-west direction

Nord-Süd-Schnitt
North-south section

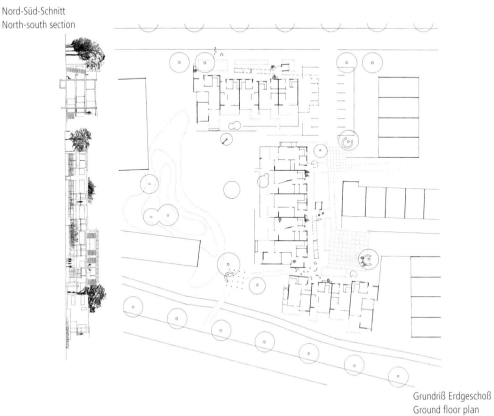

Grundriß Erdgeschoß
Ground floor plan

Umbau und Erweiterung des Kurhauses
Bad Elster, 1999

Bad Elster liegt in Sachsen, dicht an der tschechischen Grenze. Es war eines der ersten Heilbäder in Deutschland mit Großbauten im barocken Stil aus der Mitte des vorigen Jahrhunderts, die jetzt unter Denkmalschutz gestellt sind. Die Anlage konnte während der DDR-Zeit nicht ausreichend gepflegt werden. Der zentrale Innenhof diente als Betriebshof und Lagerfläche. Er wurde auf der Grundlage von Behnischs Wettbewerbsentwurf in einen zentralen Bade- und Aufenthaltsbereich umgewandelt, den «Schönen Innenhof». Das Äußere des Bestands blieb unverändert und wurde denkmalpflegerisch restauriert. Neue Funktionen wurden in und am Innenhof angesiedelt: eine gläserne Badehalle, großzügige Außenbecken, ein zentraler Eingangspavillon, Therapieeinrichtungen usw. Sie gliedern den Innenbereich, schließen ihn aber nicht ab. Die alten Gebäude bilden die Raumbegrenzungen. Auffälligstes Element ist die quadratische Badehalle mit frei geformten Becken, gläsernen Wänden und einer Decke aus beweglichen, farbigen Glaslamellen, die überraschende Lichtstimmungen im Innern wie im Äußeren erzeugen. So entstand eine Art dreidimensionaler Collage mit vielfältigen, sich überschneidenden und durchdringenden Elementen.

Conversion and extension of spa buildings
Bad Elster, 1999

Bad Elster is in Saxony, close to the Czech border. It was one of the earliest spa baths in Germany, with grand buildings in a Baroque manner built around 1850 and now listed as historic monuments. While under East German administration it was neglected, the central courtyard being used for service and storage. Because of the changing relationship with the town, Behnisch proposed to leave the grand facade facing the park while making a new entrance at what was formerly the rear, taking advantage of a small and self-important existing pavilion set just off the central axis. New social facilities are placed within the central courtyard, while new offices line its edge next to the new entrance. Being a back and informal, the courtyard had developed sporadically, without consistent order or symmetry, requiring a balanced but asymmetrical order to resolve it into a series of linked courts and pavilions. The new buildings are light and transparent in contrast with the solidity of the earlier ones, allowing maximal effect to the ground treatments and landscaping. The project is a three dimensional collage with a diverse set of overlapping and intersecting elements.

Lageplan
Site plan

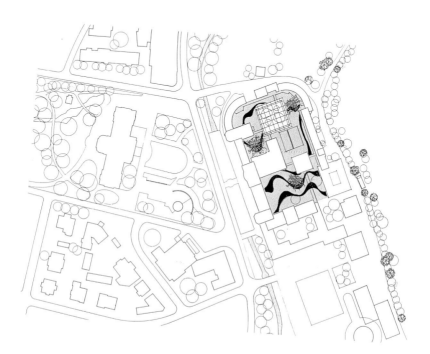

Modellaufsicht / Plan view of model

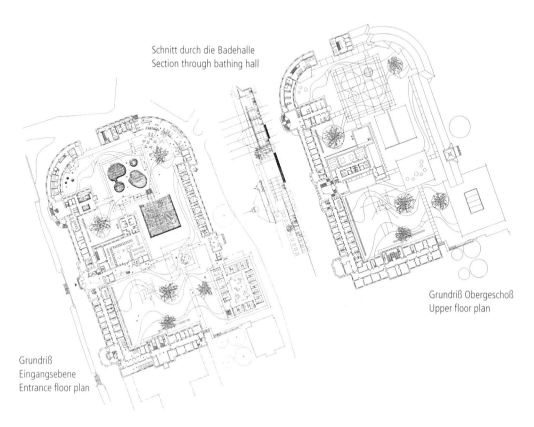

Schnitt durch die Badehalle
Section through bathing hall

Grundriß Obergeschoß
Upper floor plan

Grundriß
Eingangsebene
Entrance floor plan

Badehalle mit Außenbecken
Bathing hall with exterior pool

Schwimmbecken im Außenbereich
Exterior pool

Inneres der gläsernen Badehalle / Interior of glass bathing hall

Die lichtdurchflutete Badehalle / The light flooded bathing hall

Die Badehalle ist die architektonische Attraktion im «Schönen Hof»
The bathing hall is the architectural attraction of the "Schöner Hof"

Hallenbad
Leipzig-Grünau, 1999

Dieses Schwimmbad, in einen neuen, unter der kommunistischen Herrschaft in den siebziger/achtziger Jahren errichteten Vorort gesetzt, ist eine dringend benötigte Freizeitanlage und ein Farbtupfer in seiner monotonen Umgebung. Es entstand als Teil einer Grünanlage zwischen einer bestehenden Schule und einem Jugendklub. Der östliche Haupteingang folgt dem Verlauf der Stuttgarter Allee und dem allgemeinen Bebauungsraster, aber der Rest der Anlage schert aus und entwickelt ein eigenes, neues geometrisches System. Das rechteckige Wettkampfbecken wendet sich in eine Richtung, der Trakt mit Umkleidekabinen und Saunen in die andere, während der Freizeitbereich mit den frei geformten Becken und Rutschen sich zur dritten Seite nach Westen orientiert. Das Dach ist in einzelne Flächen aufgelöst, die sich wie Schollen über die Badefläche schieben. Dadurch ergibt sich eine bewegte Silhouette, die sich von ihrer reglementierten Nachbarbebauung abhebt. Eine einladende Treppenanlage führt über ein künstlich aufgeschüttetes Gelände an der Südwestecke zur Terrasse und zum Café im Obergeschoß mit Ausblick auf die Becken und zur Fußgängerzone. Die freie, organische, für die neuen Schwimmbäder entwickelte Architektursprache setzt sich gegen die strenge Disziplin seiner standardisierten Nachbargebäude durch und bildet eine neue Innen- und Außenlandschaft, die erforscht werden will und die Umgebung bereichert gleich einer Oase in der Wüste.

Swimming baths complex
Leipzig-Grünau, 1999

Set in a new outer suburb planned under Communist rule and built in the 1970s and 80s, this swimming bath complex adds a much needed recreation facility, and plants a touch of colour in the drabness. It was developed as part of a park between an existing school and a youth club. The eastern main entrance follows Stuttgarter Allee and the general planning grid, but the rest of the building breaks away, developing a new geometric system of its own. The rectangular competition pool cranks one way, the block of changing rooms and saunas the other, while leisure pool and water slides occupy a triangular projection to the rear. The sides are predominantly glazed, and the roof is formed in large tilted planes, giving a jagged profile which stands out among its regimented neighbours. An inviting cascade of steps leads up an artificial hill formed at the south-east corner leading to the terrace and café, a social space which overlooks both pools and street. The free, organic architectural language devised for the new baths plays against the discipline of its system-built neighbours, generating a new internal and external landscape which cries out to be explored and enriches the neighbourhood like an oasis in a desert.

Aufsicht auf die Schwimmhalle innerhalb der Plattenbausiedlung
Aerial view of the swimming hall within the housing development

Badelandschaft im Freizeitbereich / Landscape of pools in the leisure area

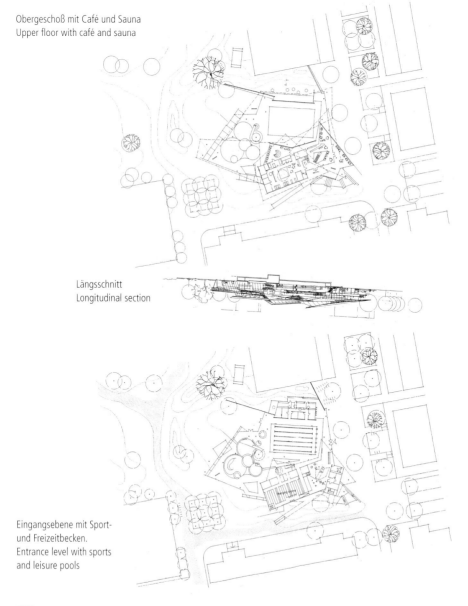

Obergeschoß mit Café und Sauna
Upper floor with café and sauna

Längsschnitt
Longitudinal section

Eingangsebene mit Sport- und Freizeitbecken.
Entrance level with sports and leisure pools

Sportbecken und Rutsche / Sports pool and slide

Whirlpool
Whirlpool

Sportbereich und Galerieebene mit Café
Sports area and gallery level with café

Kulturbauten

Deutsche Bibliothek
Frankfurt am Main, 1982
Projekt

Dieser Wettbewerbsentwurf hätte zu einem von Behnischs bedeutendsten Bauwerken führen können. Er erhielt den vierten Preis, nach einer Überarbeitungsphase den dritten, so daß man sich letztlich für die Verwirklichung eines anderen Entwurfs entschied. Das entscheidende deutsche Vorläuferprojekt war Hans Scharouns nur wenige Jahre vorher (1979) fertiggestellte Staatsbibliothek in Berlin. Behnisch & Partner schlugen ein ähnlich komplexes Gebäude vor, in dem die Funktionen frei in unterschiedlichen Winkeln zueinander gesetzt sind. Der Eingang der in der Nähe der Frankfurter City gelegenen Bibliothek soll eine wichtige Straßenkreuzung einnehmen, während der große Lesesaal an der Rückseite nach Süden zu einem Park orientiert ist. Alle Teile des Gebäudes strahlen von dieser entscheidenden Ecke aus. Die Verwaltungsräume sind in drei verbundenen Bürotrakten zusammengefaßt, die sich wie Finger spreizen. Auch der Lesesaal dahinter ist aufgefächert, seine Ebene tiefer gelegt, um als größter Raum an Höhe zu gewinnen. Die Büchermagazine liegen unsichtbar im Untergrund. Besonders bemerkenswert und im Modell sorgfältig ausgearbeitet ist das große öffentliche Foyer, das an die Innenraum-«Landschaften» von Scharouns Bibliothek erinnert. Der Raum fließt – obgleich er teilweise durch kreisförmige «Inseln» unterbrochen wird, die Vortragssäle, Ausstellungsräume und eine Cafeteria enthalten – zusammenhängend hindurch wie eine Straße.

Cultural Buildings

National Library
Frankfurt on Main, 1982
Project

This competition project might have become one of Behnisch's most important works, but gained third prize so was not built. The crucial German precedent was Hans Scharoun's Staatsbibliothek in Berlin, completed only four years earlier in 1979. Behnisch & Partners proposed a similarly complex building with functions freely articulated and set at different angles. Placed near the centre of Frankfurt, the library was to occupy an important street corner with its entrance, while the main reading room at the rear looked southward into a park. All parts of the building radiate away from the crucial corner. The administrative functions are gathered into three interlinked office wings which spread out like fingers. The reading room beyond also fans out, absorbing a drop in level to gain height as the grandest room. Books were to be stored invisibly underground. Particularly notable, and elaborately developed in the model, is the main public foyer, which recalls the internal 'landscapes' of Scharoun's library. Though partly subdivided with circular 'islands' containing auditoria, exhibitions and cafeteria, the space flows on through, street-like. The direct route from entrance to reading room is highlighted by a progression of circular ceiling wells lit by a rooflight in the floor above.

Wettbewerbsmodell / Competition model

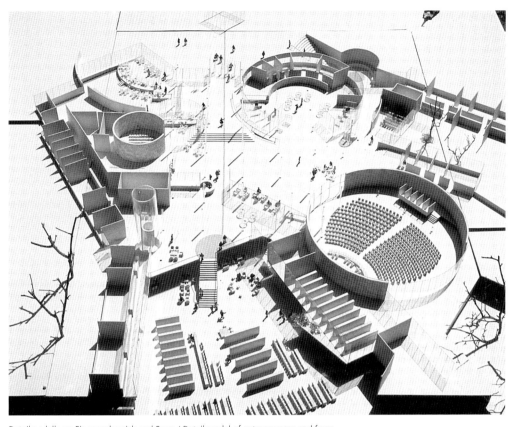
Detailmodell von Eingangsbereich und Foyer / Detail model of entrance area and foyer

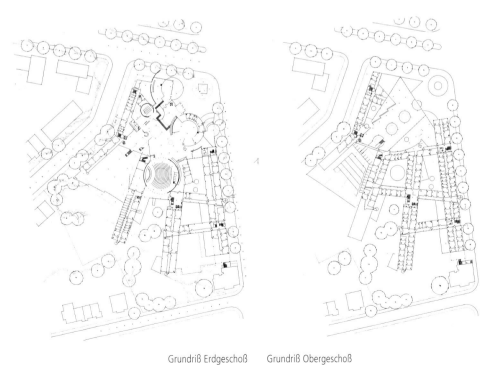

Grundriß Erdgeschoß Grundriß Obergeschoß
Ground floor plan   Upper floor plan

Hysolar-Institut der Universität Stuttgart
Stuttgart-Vaihingen, 1987

Als Forschungsinstitut für Solarenergie sieht dieses Gebäude dementsprechend wie ein Laborgerät aus. Es wurde innerhalb kurzer Zeit mit einem geringen Etat realisiert, daher war es geboten, vorgefertigte Container für die Laboratorien zu verwenden. Die beiden Trakte werden von verschiedenen Gruppen genutzt: der östliche von Angehörigen der Universität, der westliche von unabhängigen Forschungsteams. Die Schrägstellung ermöglichte es, die verglaste Halle zum Haupteingang und zur Sonne zu öffnen, während der vorgeschobene Westtrakt an der Nordseite geschlossen ist, weil darin Wasserstoff erzeugt wird. Um die Auswirkungen potentieller Explosionen zu begrenzen, ist dieser Raum mit einem leichten Dach und Wänden versehen, die gegebenenfalls ausbrechen würden. Elemente wie die Schrägsprossen der Verglasung und die verschobenen Fenster haben keine pragmatische Begründung. Die spektakulärste formale Geste ist ein rotes Stahlrohr, das an der Nordseite des Gebäudes ausbricht, durch die Halle stößt und aus der verglasten Südseite herausragt. Dieses Element ist fast ausschließlich rhetorisch, denn seine einzige praktische Funktion besteht darin, ein kurzes Ende des Daches zu tragen. Institute dieser Art zeichnen sich im allgemeinen durch betrübliche Langeweile aus und unterdrücken mit ihren standardisierten Rasterkisten jede spezielle Aussage über ihre Funktion. Dieser Bau ist zumindest provokativ und einprägsam; er vermittelt etwas von der aufregenden Pionierarbeit, die in ihm geleistet wird.

Hysolar research institute
Stuttgart-Vaihingen, 1987

A research institute concerned with solar energy, this building looks appropriately like a laboratory test-rig. It was completed quickly on a tight budget, so there were advantages in using factory-made containers for laboratory rooms. The two wings are used by different groups: the east by university faculties, the west by independent groups. Their oblique placing allows the glazed hall to open up towards main entrance and the sun, while the projecting west-wing room at the north end is isolated because its equipment produces hydrogen. To limit the effects of an explosion, this room has a light roof and walls which would blow out. Elements such as the sloping glazing mullions and twisted windows are not pragmatically justifiable, and the most extravagant formal gesture is a red steel tube which bursts from the ground north of the building, traverses the hall, and projects through the glazed south end. This is almost entirely rhetorical, for its only practical function is to support a short tail of roof. Most other institutes of this kind are lamentably dull, repressing everything special about their function within a standard grid-planned box. This one is at least provocative and memorable, conveying the excitement of the frontier-pushing work which takes place within.

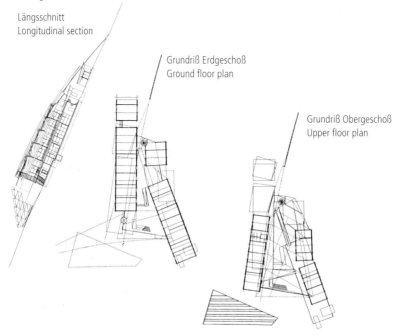

Längsschnitt
Longitudinal section

Grundriß Erdgeschoß
Ground floor plan

Grundriß Obergeschoß
Upper floor plan

Ansicht von Süden / View from the south

Hallenverglasung von Süden / Hall glazing seen from the south

Steg und Erschließungsflure
Bridge and access galleries

Übergang von vorgefertigten
Raumzellen, Hallendach und
Glasabschluß
Transition between prefabricated room cells, hall roof and glazing

Ansicht von Norden
View from the north

Hallenraum im Obergeschoß / Hall space on upper floor

Universitätsbibliothek
Eichstätt, 1987

University library
Eichstätt, 1987

Die Kleinstadt Eichstätt, im malerischen Tal der Altmühl zwischen München und Nürnberg gelegen, ist Bistum und Sitz einer katholischen Universität. Die neue Bibliothek steht auf einem weitläufigen Grundstück in einer Flußaue am Stadtrand und ist horizontal ausgelegt mit einer maximalen Höhe von drei Geschossen. Da keine Nachbarbebauung vorhanden ist, konnte das Gebäude frei nach den darin stattfindenden Funktionen und mit Ausblick in alle Richtungen geplant werden. Das Programm umfaßte Fakultätsräume und Lehrbereiche sowie die Bibliothek mit allen dazugehörigen Einrichtungen. Diese funktionale Dichotomie, die eigentlich zwei unabhängige Gebäude erfordert hätte, ist am ausgeführten Komplex ablesbar. In drei nach Norden und Osten orientierten dreigeschossigen Trakten liegen die Fakultätsräume, während das große, nach Süden ausstrahlende Element und der eingeschossige Westflügel den Lesesaal und die übrigen Bibliotheksräume enthalten. Von außen ist der Wechsel im Maßstab zwischen Verwaltung und Lesesaal an der Fassadenbehandlung erkennbar; der Lesesaal ist in voller Höhe verglast, sein überstehendes Dach wird von schlanken Stützen getragen. Im Gegensatz dazu benötigt das große, dem Publikum nicht zugängliche Büchermagazin keine Front zur Außenwelt und ist mit Erde überschüttet und bepflanzt. Bibliothek und Fakultätsräume begegnen sich in der großen, von Norden belichteten Halle, deren geometrische Trennung ihre relative Unabhängigkeit zum Ausdruck bringt.

A small town in the picturesque valley of the river Altmühl between Munich and Nuremberg, Eichstätt is a bishopric and has a catholic university. Its new library stands on a riverside meadow just outside the town, generously sited to spread horizontally with a maximum height of three storeys. Lacking near neighbours, it develops from inner requirements and exploits views in all directions. The programme included faculty offices and teaching spaces as well as the library and its facilities. This functional dichotomy, which could have given rise to independent buildings, is articulated in the completed complex. Triple three-storey wings to north and east contain the faculties, while the large radial element to south and the single storey west wing contain reading room and library offices. Externally the change in scale between offices and reading room is visible in the facade treatment, the reading room glazing running full height, its projecting roof carried on slender columns. Conversely, the large bookstore which is not part of the public experience and requires no face to the world, is buried in the ground. Library and faculties meet in the north-lit hall, the geometric disjunction making their relative independence felt.

Die Situation des Bibliotheksgebäudes außerhalb der Kernstadt
Setting of the library building outside the town centre

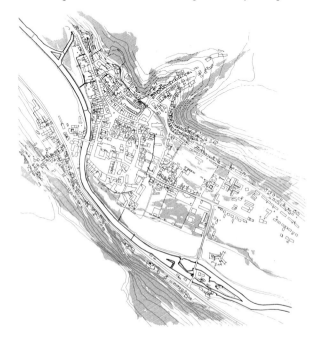

Ansicht von Süd-Osten / View from the south-east

Grundriß Obergeschoß mit Galerieebene des Lesesaals und Büroriegeln der Fakultäten
Upper floor plan with reading room gallery and faculties' office wings

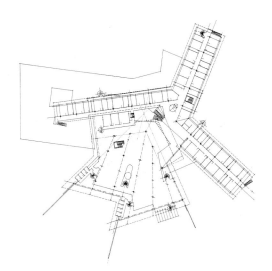

Nord-Süd-Schnitt
North-south section

Grundriß Erdgeschoß mit Verwaltungsbereich, Büchermagazin und Lesesaal
Ground floor plan with administrative area, book-stacks and reading space

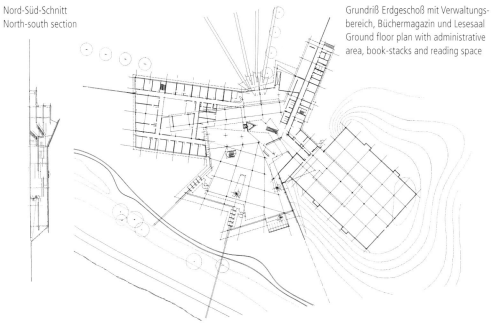

Blick von der Halle in den Lesesaal / View from hall into reading room

Treppenverbindungen in der Halle
Stair connections in hall

Leseplätze im Süden an der Altmühl / Reading area in the south on the Altmühl river

Spindeltreppe
Spiral stair

Süd-West-Ecke des Lesesaals
South-west corner of the reading room

Museum für Post und Kommunikation
Frankfurt am Main, 1990

Das Postmuseum gehört zu einer Reihe von Museumsbauten am Südufer des Mains, einem Stadtgebiet, das im 19. Jahrhundert mit Privatvillen bebaut wurde und nach dem Willen der Stadtplaner seinen «villenähnlichen» Charakter bewahren sollte. Der Wettbewerb bot die Option, die auf dem Gelände vorhandene Villa entweder zu erhalten oder abzureißen. Behnisch entschied sich für die Erhaltung und nutzte den Altbau für Verwaltungsräume und die Bibliothek. Diese Entscheidung war der Ausgangspunkt für alles Nachfolgende; doch anstatt die Planung einzuschränken, erwiesen sich die Zwänge als Vorzüge. Auf der rechten Seite des Grundstücks wurde ein neuer Baukörper hinzugefügt, der Eingangsbereich und Ausstellungsräume enthält. Mit seiner bescheidenen Stirnseite beeinträchtigt er den Maßstab der vorhandenen Häuserreihe nicht. Größere Ausstellungsflächen konnten nur unter dem Villengarten gewonnen werden; die bestehenden Bäume blieben erhalten, indem man die Wurzelballen in Betonzylinder setzte. Um diese Trommeln angeordnete Deckenlichter öffen das Untergeschoß zum Himmel; der Geniestreich war jedoch der Einfall, mit einem Luftraum unter einen schrägen Glaszylinder die unter- und oberirdischen Ebenen großzügig miteinander zu verbinden. Die Verkehrsführung ist erfreulich klar, denn vom Eingang führen Treppenläufe bis zum obersten Ausstellungsbereich, während eine diagonale Treppe im großen Lichtraum die Besucher zum Ausstellungssaal im Untergeschoß leitet. Die mit Aluminium verkleidete Außenhaut und die von Antennen strotzenden Dachaufbauten spiegeln den technischen Charakter des Inhalts und das in die Zukunft gerichtete Engagement der Post.

Post and Communications Museum
Frankfurt on Main, 1990

The Post Museum is one of a series of museums running along the south bank of the river Main, an area built up in the 19th century as private villas, and designated by the city planners to remain 'villa-like'. The competition left optional whether to preserve the existing villa on the site or to demolish it. Behnisch decided on preservation, using the old building as offices and library. From this decision everything followed, but instead of limiting the design, the constraints became virtues. A second villa-like structure was added to the right, serving as main entrance and providing exhibition space, but limited in size to maintain the scale of the row. Further exhibition space could only be made by digging under the garden, avoiding existing trees by setting their roots in concrete cylinders. Rooflights around these drums open the basement to the sky, but the masterstroke was the creation of a semicircular void under a tilted cylinder of glass. This links all levels and creates a heart to the building, bringing the linearity of the new wing to an appropriate termination. The circulation is commendably clear, for running stairs proceed from entrance to top gallery, while a diagonal stair in the great well leads visitors to the big gallery in the basement. The visible superstructure, clad in aluminium and bristling with antennae, reflects the technical character of the contents and the continuing progressive ambitions of the post company.

Das Postmuseum mit der Skyline der Stadt
Post Museum with skyline

Lageplan
Site plan

Altbau und Neubau am Main / Old and new buildings of the museum along the Main river

Zugangsbereich am Schaumainkai
Entrance area on Schaumainkai

Der Glaszylinder vom Gartenhof / Glass cylinder seen from garden court

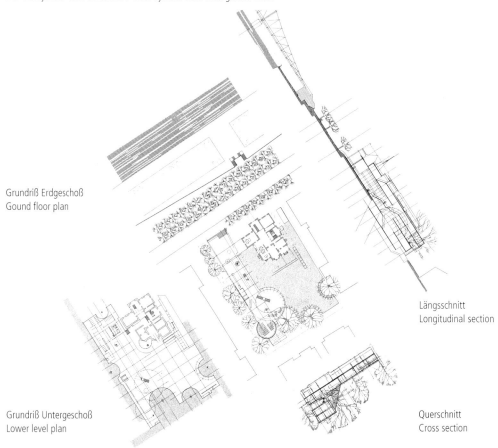

Grundriß Erdgeschoß
Gound floor plan

Grundriß Untergeschoß
Lower level plan

Längsschnitt
Longitudinal section

Querschnitt
Cross section

Die Ausstellungsflächen im Untergeschoß / Lower level exhibition areas

Blick durch die Verglasung des Kegels auf die Villa / View of villa through glass cone

Im Luftraum der Halle treffen alle Ebenen zusammen / All levels meet in the hall's open space

Blick vom zweiten
Obergeschoß in die Halle
View from the second
level into the hall

Akademie der Künste Berlin-Brandenburg
Berlin, 2002

Nach Fertigstellung wird die neue Akademie der Künste wohl zu Behnischs bedeutendsten Bauwerken gehören. Die Akademie kehrt damit an ihren Sitz aus der Vorkriegszeit an der Südseite des Pariser Platzes zurück, wo die Straße Unter den Linden auf das Brandenburger Tor trifft. Das lange, schmale Grundstück geht durch bis in die Behrenstraße und ist – abgesehen von einem öden Hof im Osten – von Brandmauern umgeben. Eine Reihe massiver Ausstellungshallen steht an der erinnerungsträchtigen Achse, welche die Kriegszerstörungen überstanden hat. Behnisch gewann den internen Wettbewerb mit einem Entwurf, der den problematischen Gegebenheiten Rechnung trägt. Im ersten Stadium enthielt er Neubauten auf beiden Seiten; die Reduzierung des Etats forderte jedoch schließlich eine Konzentration auf das Hauptgebäude am Pariser Platz. Darin sind die Repräsentationsräume und in mehreren unterirdischen Geschossen das Archiv enthalten. Die alten Ausstellungshallen in der Mitte des Grundstücks werden für ihre ursprüngliche Verwendung wieder hergestellt; hinzu kommen ein Skulpturengarten auf Ebene des ersten Obergeschosses sowie ein Studiotheater im Untergeschoß. Östlich vom Ausstellungsbereich liegen ein zweigeschossiges Foyer und das Restaurant, im Westen befindet sich ein dreigeschossiger Bürotrakt. Die Konstruktion ist leicht und offen, weitgehend verglast, um Helligkeit und Ausblick zu gewährleisten; zur Halle sind die einzelnen Ebenen in unterschiedlichen Winkeln begrenzt, um den Raum vertikal zu öffnen und Sichtbeziehungen zu erleichtern. Behnisch wollte die Transparenz bis zum Platz fortsetzen, geriet damit jedoch in Konflikt mit den Bauvorschriften, die massive Wände forderten. Er argumentierte – schließlich mit Erfolg –, daß es möglich sei, den Rhythmus und die Proportionen des Vorgängerbaus aufzunehmen, aber auf dessen archaische Bausubstanz zu verzichten.

New building for the Berlin-Brandenburg Arts Academy
Berlin, 2002

When complete, this will be among Behnisch's most significant buildings and one that received much personal attention. Following reunification the Academy decided to return to its pre-war site on the south side of Pariser Platz, the square at which Unter den Linden meets Brandenburg Gate. The long thin plot runs from the square to Behrenstrasse, its sides hemmed-in by party walls except for a shallow court to east. A line of massively built exhibition halls running down the axis had survived wartime destruction, and carries an important memory. Behnisch won the competition with an elaborate series of buildings exploiting these difficult conditions. At first this involved new buildings at both ends, but a reduced budget meant financially concentrating on the Pariser Platz front. This contains the main representative functions above ground and a multi-layer archive in the basement. The old exhibition halls in the middle will be restored for their original purpose, but with an added sculpture court above the first to create a new heart at first floor and a studio theatre in the basement. East of the galleries, with a view to the side court, is a two-level foyer and restaurant, to west a high-level three-floor office wing. The structure is lightweight and open, much glazed for light and views, with floors cut back at varied angles to open the space vertically and ease connections. Behnisch wanted to continue the transparency into the square, but ran into difficulties with a planning policy demanding massive walls. He argued – in the end successfully – that it is possible to reflect the rhythm and proportions of the former building without repeating its archaic substance.

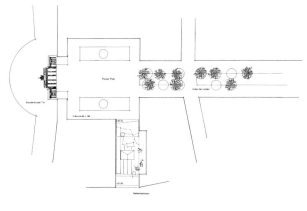

Die Lage des Akademiegebäudes
am Pariser Platz
Site of the Academy building on
Pariser Platz

Die Fassade am Pariser Platz / Facade on Pariser Platz

Blick von Süden über die alten Ausstellungshallen auf den Kopfbau
View from the south across the old exhibition halls toward the main building

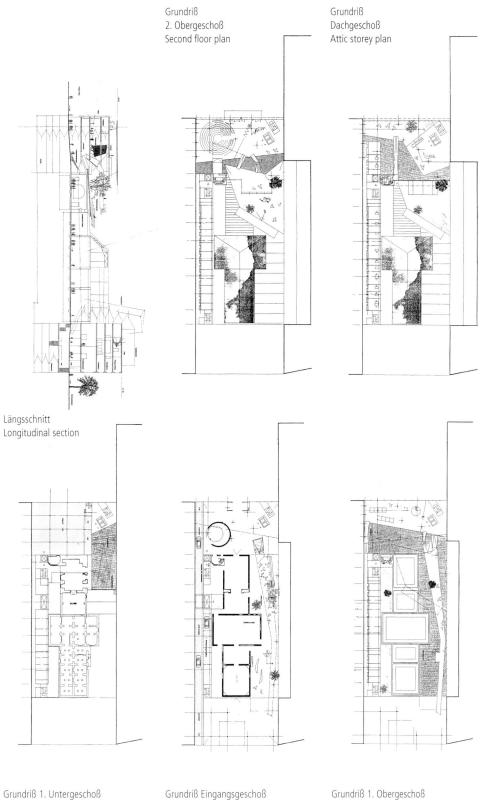

Grundriß 2. Obergeschoß
Second floor plan

Grundriß Dachgeschoß
Attic storey plan

Längsschnitt
Longitudinal section

Grundriß 1. Untergeschoß
First lower level plan

Grundriß Eingangsgeschoß
Entrance level plan

Grundriß 1. Obergeschoß
First floor plan

Schnittmodell von Osten / Section model from the east

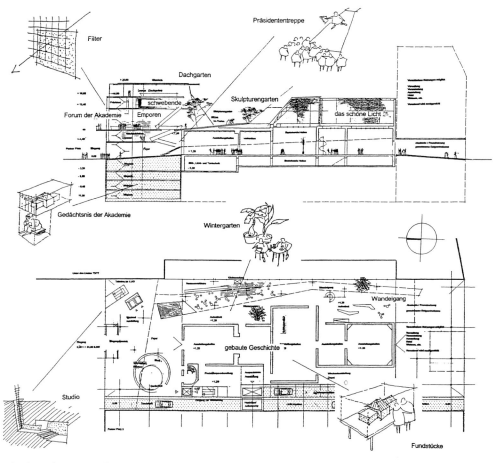

Architektonische Orte / Focal points

Theater- und Konzerthalle
Bristol, 1996
Projekt

Dieses Projekt einer Konzerthalle und eines Tanztheaters wäre der erste Bau von Behnisch in England geworden, die Lottomittel dafür wurden jedoch im letzten Stadium verweigert. Der Bauplatz im Stadtzentrum neben dem alten Hafen bot eine spektakuläre Situation, aber auch viele Planungsprobleme. Die geforderten Hauptbereiche waren eine Konzerthalle mit 2000 Plätzen, eine kleinere Halle für Tanz- und Ballettveranstaltungen mit 500 Plätzen, ein Probensaal und ein öffentliches Foyer sowie Restaurants. Die großen Säle wurden als formgebende Wahrzeichen der gesamten Anlage gestaltet, ebenso wichtig war jedoch die Raumabfolge vom New World Square durch das Gebäude zur Hafenfront, die durch eine neue diagonale Achse zur großen Halle aufgewertet werden sollte. Der kleinere Saal ist zu einem benachbarten Gebäude ausgerichtet, so entsteht zwischen den beiden ein komplexer und durchlässiger Foyerraum, der durchsetzt ist mit Treppen als richtungweisenden Elementen, mit Brücken und Galerien darüber und gekrönt von einem schräg abfallenden Glasdach. Die Halle ähnelte zunächst Scharouns Berliner Philharmonie; weitere Untersuchungen führten jedoch zu einem stärker vertikal ausgerichteten Entwurf und zu größerer Flexibilität von Bühne und Sitzplätzen. Der im großen Winkel zum Wasser geöffnete Neubau in Bristol wäre von den Hügeln der Umgebung sichtbar und ein leuchtendes Juwel mit kontrastierenden transparenten und reflektierenden Außenflächen in der Stadt gewesen. Durch ihre Arbeit mit Modellen gelangten die Architekten zu einer Außenform, die dem Innern nur annähernd entspricht; sie legten den Schwerpunkt auf eine Folge gefalteter Dächer und Wandflächen, ohne zwischen beiden zu unterscheiden. Das Gebäude hätte wie ein Chamäleon durch Veränderung von Maßstab und Transparenz auf die unterschiedlichen Richtungen reagiert.

Arts centre
Bristol, 1996
Project

This project for a concert hall would have been the first Behnisch building in Britain, but lottery-funding was refused at the last stage. The city-centre site next to the old harbour offered dramatic views but presented many planning difficulties. The main spaces demanded were a concert hall seating 2000, a more intimate hall for dance and ballet seating 500, a rehearsal hall, and public foyers and restaurants. The main halls were articulated as shaping landmarks within the whole, but equally important was the spatial progression from New World Square through the building to the harbour front, celebrated with a new diagonal axis set up for the main hall. The small hall aligned itself with an adjacent building, so between the two a complex and transparent foyer space developed, laced with stairs placed as directional elements, with bridges and galleries over, and topped by a sloping glass roof. The hall was modelled on Scharoun's Berlin Philharmonie, but exploratory work led to a more vertical design, and since it was to be used for many different kinds of concert including pop, also greater flexibility of stage and seating. Open to a wide angle of water, the Bristol building would have been seen from the surrounding hills, and the architects made it a glowing jewel in the city, with contrasting transparent and reflective surfaces. Working with models, they devised an external form that followed the interior only approximately, relying on a series of folded roof and wall plates, not differentiating between the two. The building would have responded chameleon-like to different directions, changing in scale and transparency.

Blick über die Wasserflächen der Hafenanlagen
View across the reflective basin

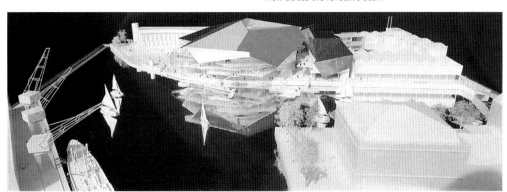

Grundriß Erdgeschoß mit öffentlicher Halle
Ground floor plan with public concourse

Grundriß Obergeschoß mit Konzerthalle und Foyers
Upper floor plan with concert hall and foyers

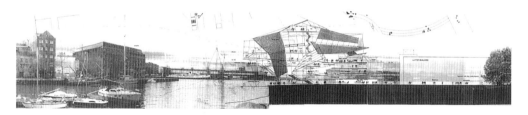

Schnitt durch die Säle / Section through the main halls

Schnitt durch die Halle / Section through hall

Blick vom Stadtzentrum auf den Neubau
View of new construction from the city centre

Dachlandschaft
Roofscape

Innenraum der Konzerthalle / Interior of concert hall

Lothar-Günther-Buchheim-Museum
Bernried, 2000

Lothar-Günther Buchheim ist nicht nur der Verfasser des international erfolgreich verfilmten Romans «Das Boot», der Geschichte eines Unterseeboots und seiner Besatzung im Zweiten Weltkrieg, sondern auch ein passionierter Sammler von Kunst und Kuriositäten. Das Gebäude ist zur Ausstellung seiner ungewöhnlichen Sammlung bestimmt, die bisher in verschiedenen Villen und Nebengebäuden untergebracht war. Die Exponate reichen von wertvoller Kunst des 20. Jahrhunderts bis zu Volkskunstobjekten und sind nicht nach üblichen Kategorien, sondern nach Buchheims privatem System klassifiziert, das ihnen eine andere Bedeutung verleiht. Sein «Kuriositätenkabinett» geht auf die ersten Museen des 18. Jahrhunderts zurück, und bei seinem «Buchheim total» handelt es sich um einen persönlichen Bericht. Das Gelände am Südwestufer des Starnberger Sees bei München ist ein Naturpark, für das ein Gebäude entlang einer zentralen waagerechten Achse entwickelt wurde, die am Eingang beginnt und an einem Aussichtssteg über dem Seeufer endet. Links und nördlich von dieser Achse liegen die Ausstellungsräume für Malerei und Bildhauerei. Kunstwerke, die Dunkelheit erfordern, sind auf der unteren Ebene in den Hang gesetzt, während andere nach vorn heraustreten und kontrolliertem Tageslicht ausgesetzt sind. Südlich und rechts von der Achse liegen weitere offene Bereiche, einschließlich einer kreisförmigen Cafeteria; die allgemeine Durchlässigkeit bedeutet jedoch, daß alles Teil einer räumlichen Sequenz ist, die zu Entdeckungen einlädt. Ausblicke in die Landschaft werden genutzt. Das Gebäude ist leicht und zurückhaltend geplant, um die Dramatik der Umgebung für sich sprechen zu lassen.

Lothar-Günther Buchheim Museum
Bernried, 2000

Lothar-Günther Buchheim is the author of 'Das Boot', the story of a Second-World-War submarine and its crew which became an internationally famous film, but he is also a passionate collector of art and curiosities. The building is intended to put his unusual collection, which grew into various villas and out-buildings, together on public display. The exhibits range from valuable 20th century art to folk objects, and are classified not according to normal categories but on Buchheim's private system which gives them a different meaning. His 'cabinet of curiosities', harks back to the first museums of the 18th century, and his 'Buchheim Total' is a personal memoir. The site on the south-west shore of the Starnberger See near Munich is a natural park, and a linear building was developed along a level central spine which begins with the entrance and ends in a pier overlooking the lake. To left and north of this spine are galleries for painting and sculpture. Works requiring darkness are set back into the hill at a lower level, while others emerge from it, exposed to controlled daylight. To south and right of the spine are more open areas, including the circular cafeteria, but the general transparency means that everything is part of a fluid progression, offering voyages of discovery. Views of the landscape are exploited and the building is intended to be light and unobtrusive, letting the drama of the setting speak for itself.

Das «Museum der Phantasie» am Starnberger See / The "Museum of Fantasy" on Starnberg Lake

Modellfoto. Süd-Ost-Ansicht / Model. South-east view

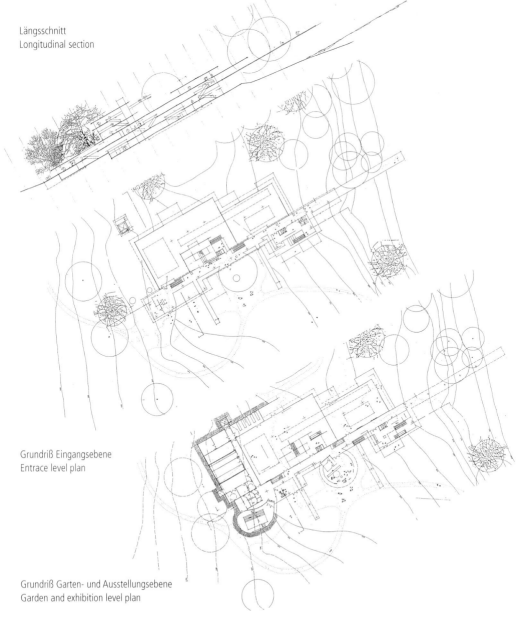

Längsschnitt
Longitudinal section

Grundriß Eingangsebene
Entrace level plan

Grundriß Garten- und Ausstellungsebene
Garden and exhibition level plan

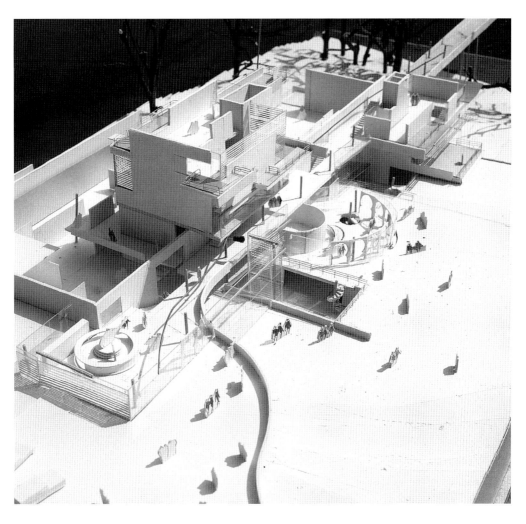

Schrägaufsicht auf das Modell ohne Dach
Angled view of model without roof

Modellaufsicht mit Steg über dem See
View with pier over lake

Staatsarchiv
Kopenhagen, 2004

Dieses riesige Gebäude, das Ergebnis eines internationalen Wettbewerbs von 1996, wird eine Grünfläche zwischen dem Stadtzentrum und den südlichen Vororten einnehmen, nach Norden zur Universität orientiert und zwischen große Straßen und die erhöht geführte Bahnlinie gesetzt sein. Ein kleiner vorhandener Bach dient zur Bildung eines spiegelnden Sees, aus dem die Nordseite des Gebäudes aufsteigen wird. Die Archive sind in in einer Gruppe geschlossener Türme im Osten des Grundstücks untergebracht, in Quadern unterschiedlicher Größe und Höhe, die auf einem standardisierten Lagerelement basieren und um einen gemeinsamen Fahrstuhlschacht angeordnet sind. Sie bilden eine plastische Komposition, deren Profil sich je nach Blickrichtung ständig verändert und das Licht zu unterschiedlichen Zeiten einfängt, aber auch eine Erweiterung in jedem beliebigen Maßstab zuläßt. Auf der unteren Ebene erstreckt sich der Bau auf der Westseite zu einer Reihe von Lesesälen mit offenem Grundriß, die in viele verbundene Ebenen terrassiert und nach außen verglast sind. Dadurch entsteht eine offene «Landschaft» zum gemeinsamen Lesen, ähnlich wie in Scharouns Berliner Staatsbibliothek. Der Haupteingang ist nach Westen zur Bahn orientiert. Eine lange, flache Erdrampe führt zu einer großzügigen Halle, die Garderoben und eine Cafeteria enthält; Treppen führen aufwärts zu den Leseräumen. Darüber sind die Verwaltungsbüros in schmalen Bändern zusammengefaßt, deren unterste Ebene das zentrale, von oben belichtete Volumen abschließt und deren obere Geschosse in einem auskragenden Flügel mit Ausblick nach Norden und Süden den Eingang betonen. In der Detailplanung dienen die vielen Ecken und Winkel zur Abgrenzung der Teile und zur Identifizierung mit dem Ort sowie zur Vermeidung monotoner Wiederholung und Überdimensionierung, durch die große Komplexe dieser Art so häufig beeinträchtigt werden.

National and Provincial Archives building
Copenhagen, 2004

This enormous building, result of an international competition in 1996, will occupy a green area between city centre and southern suburbs, looking north towards the university. Placed between major road and elevated railway, it takes advantage of a small existing stream to form a reflecting lake out of which the north side of the building will grow. The archives are contained in a group of blind towers placed east on the site, boxes of different sizes and heights based on a standard storage unit and gathered around a common stack of lifts. They form a sculptural composition, varying in profile from different directions and catching the light at different times, but also facilitating expansion at any required scale. At low level the building expands on its west side into a series of open plan reading-rooms, terraced in many linked levels and glazed to the outside world. This will produce an open 'landscape' of shared reading as with Scharoun's Staatsbibliothek in Berlin. The main entrance faces west towards the railway station. A long slow ramp leads to a generous hall providing cloakrooms and cafeteria, with stairs on up to reading levels. The administrative offices form narrow bands above the reading rooms, the lowest level defining the edge of the central top lit volume, the upper ones forming a projecting wing to help define the entrance, with views north and south. In detailed planning the many corners and shifts of angle serve to differentiate between the parts and to bestow a sense of place, avoiding the excessive repetition and overscaling which so often mars large complexes of this kind.

Die Silhouette von Süd-Westen / Skyline from south-west

Modellaufsicht von Norden / View of model from north

Lageplan
Site plan

Wettbewerbsmodell. Herbst 1996 / Competition model. Autumn 1996

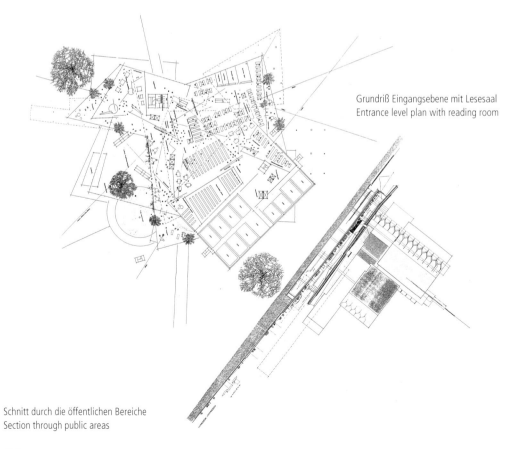

Grundriß Eingangsebene mit Lesesaal
Entrance level plan with reading room

Schnitt durch die öffentlichen Bereiche
Section through public areas

Ansicht von Westen / View from the west

Ansicht von Süden
View from the south

Verwaltungs- und Industriebauten

Herbert-Keller-Haus, Landesgeschäftsstelle des Diakonischen Werkes
Stuttgart, 1984

Das Herbert-Keller-Haus ist die Geschäftsstelle der evangelischen Wohlfahrtseinrichtung, die sich der Minderbemittelten, Behinderten, Drogenabhängigen und anderer sozial schwacher Gruppen annimmt. Es steht im Neubaugebiet Löwentorzentrum nördlich vom Stuttgarter Hauptbahnhof und unterlag den Beschränkungen eines phantasielosen Bebauungsplans, der ein festgelegtes Stützenraster, abgeleitet von zusammenhängenden Garagenflächen, vorgab. Trotzdem und auch der seelenlosen und wenig gegliederten Nachbarbebauung zum Trotz gelang Behnisch & Partnern ein bemerkenswert lebendiges und freundliches Gebäude, das dem menschlichen Maßstab entspricht. Obgleich sie gezwungen waren, die Bürotrakte in die vom Bebauungsplan vorgeschriebenen Zonen zu stellen, durchbrachen sie das System, wo immer es möglich war: Sie variierten die Höhe der Trakte, sie setzten begehbare Terrassen darauf, betonten das Café im Erdgeschoß und die Besprechungsräume im ersten Obergeschoß als unregelmäßige, auskragende Volumen und konzentrierten den ganzen Bau auf einen treibhausähnlichen Innenhof mit zu öffnendem Glasdach. Anstelle öder Flure errichteten sie ein System aus großzügigen Sozialbereichen als Warteräume und für gelegentliche Kontakte, indem sie die Ecken öffneten und häufige Ausblicke ermöglichten. Die Fassaden werden durch Sonnenschutzelemente belebt, die der Klimakontrolle dienen. Inmitten seiner langweiligen kommerziellen Nachbarn verleiht dieses Gebäude einer Stimme Gehör, die von Freiheit und Individualität kündet.

Commercial Buildings

Regional headquarters of the Diakonisches Werk religious charity
Stuttgart, 1984

Herbert Keller Haus is the office building for a religious charity which cares for the poor, the sick, the addicted and other unlucky social groups. It is part of the redeveloped Löwenzentrum just north of Stuttgart's main railway station, built within the straitjacket of an unimaginative master plan which included a predetermined column grid set by the underground garage beneath. Despite this, and despite being surrounded by soulless and box-like neighbours, Behnisch & Partners managed to produce a remarkably lively and friendly building which recovers the human scale. Obliged to put the office wings within the zones prescribed by the masterplan, they broke away from the system wherever they could, varying the heights of the wings, topping them with usable terraces, articulating the ground-floor café and first-floor conference rooms as projecting irregular volumes, and centring the whole on a greenhouse-like atrium with opening glass roof. In place of dreary corridors they created a network of generous social spaces for waiting and casual contact, opening up corners and allowing frequent views out. The facades are enlivened by sun-shading devices that combine kinetic sculpture with environmental control. Amid its dull commercial neighbours, the building strikes a resonant note of freedom and individuality.

Gesamtlageplan Löwentorzentrum
General site plan Löwentorzentrum

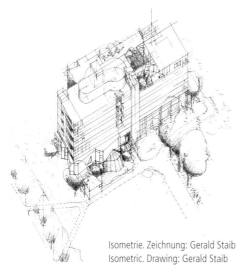

Isometrie. Zeichnung: Gerald Staib
Isometric. Drawing: Gerald Staib

Detail der Südfassade / Detail of south facade

Ansicht von Süden / View from the south

Cafeteria / Café

Grundriß 5. Obergeschoß
Fifth floor plan

Grundriß 3. Obergeschoß
Third floor plan

Grundriß 1. Obergeschoß
First floor plan

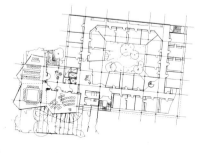

Schnitt
Section

Grundriß Erdgeschoß
Ground floor plan

Büroräume am grünen Innenhof / Office spaces around the green courtyard

Blick von der Eingangshalle in den Innenhof
View from entrance hall into courtyard

Ansicht von Nordosten
View from north-east

Leybold-Werk
Alzenau bei Frankfurt am Main, 1987

Dieser große Industriebau zur Produktion von Mikroelektronik-Elementen hat eine zentrale, vom nördlichen Eingang ausgehende Verkehrsachse. Östlich davon liegt ein Labortrakt, gefolgt von mehreren Produktionshallen, die durch Innenhöfe voneinander abgegrenzt werden. Im Westen befinden sich halbkreisförmige Büroräume und der große Halbkreis des Casinos. Am Außenrand der Produktionshallen verläuft eine Straße zur Anlieferung, während der Bereich auf der Büroseite als Grünfläche mit einem See gestaltet ist, über dem die Bauten wie riesige Erker zum Genießen der Aussicht schweben. Die 26 m breiten und 80 m tiefen Produktionshallen sind horizontal angelegt mit außenliegenden Stahlkonstruktionen und Versorgungsleitungen, so daß innen durchgehende, flache Decken ermöglicht wurden. Im Gegensatz dazu haben die Verkehrsachse und die Bürotrakte ein feingliedriges Beton-Tragwerk; die halbkreisförmigen Grundrisse verleihen allen Büros eine starke Identität und reduzieren ihren Maßstab. Auch das System der Versorgungsleitungen ist hier ein anderes, denn während es sich bei den Produktionshallen um absolute Reinräume mit streng gefilterter Klimatisierung handelt, betretbar über eine dekontaminierte Zone in einem niedrigen Verbindungstrakt, können die Fenster in den Büros geöffnet werden. Die Sonneneinstrahlung wird durch außenliegende Blenden geregelt. Die viergeschossige Masse der Bürorundlinge wird optisch durch Verglasung des ersten Obergeschosses und Freilegung der Konstruktion reduziert. Das Erdgeschoß ist völlig offen und ermöglicht den Mitarbeitern in den dahinterliegenden Produktionshallen einen Ausblick. Aufgrund zahlreicher Unterbrechungen ist die große Länge der Achse niemals spürbar. Sie taucht nur am Nordende unverhüllt auf, kragt dort abgeschrägt aus und bildet eine Vorfahrt, wo die Besucher aussteigen können. Die kreisförmige Grundrißgeometrie wiederholt sich in der niedrigen Eingangshalle, die als Empfangs- und Ausstellungsraum dient und von der aus Rolltreppen zur Verkehrsachse im ersten Obergeschoß führen.

Leybold factory
Alzenau near Frankfurt on Main, 1987

This large factory building for the production of microelectronics has a central circulation spine running back from its northern entrance. To east is a laboratory wing, followed by a series of production halls divided by courts. To west are semicircular offices and the larger semicircle of the works restaurant. At their outer edge the production halls meet a service road for loading and unloading, while the territory on the office side is garden and lake, the buildings projecting like giant bay-windows to enjoy the views. The 26 m wide production halls are linear with external steel structure and servicing to allow flat ceilings within. In contrast, the circulation spine and offices have a small-span concrete frame, the semicircular layouts giving each office a strong identity and reducing the scale. The servicing strategy also changes, for while production halls are scrupulously clean with stringently filtered air-conditioning, being entered via a decontamination zone in a low connecting wing, the offices are allowed opening windows, solar gain being controlled by external blinds. The four-storey mass of the office bays is reduced visually by glazing the first-floor and exposing the structure. It is left fully open at ground level to allow production workers in the halls behind a view out. With its many interruptions, the great length of the spine is never felt. It emerges nakedly only at the north end, cut on the skew and projecting to form a *porte cochère* where visitors are dropped off. The circular plan geometry is repeated in the low entrance hall, which serves as reception and showroom, connected by escalators to the first-floor circulation axis.

Produktionshallen und Labor von Osten
Production halls and laboratory from the east

Blick über den Luftraum einer Halle auf Arbeitsplätze in einem der Rundlinge
View of work areas in one of the round volumes across the open space of a void

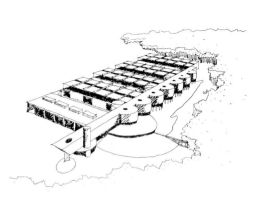

Isometrie der kompletten Anlage
Isometric of entire complex

Empfangsbereich in der Eingangshalle
Reception area in the entrance hall

Grundriß Eingangsgeschoß
Entrance floor plan

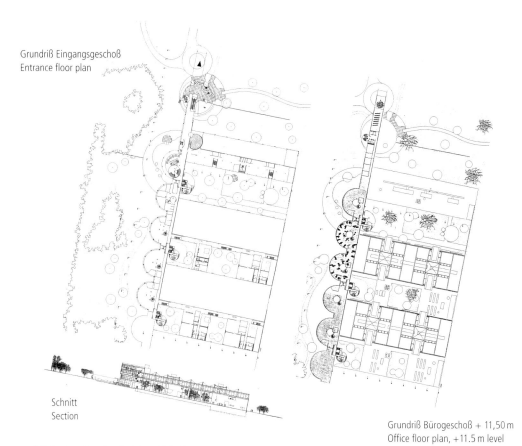

Schnitt
Section

Grundriß Bürogeschoß + 11,50 m
Office floor plan, +11.5 m level

Hallenbereich in einem der Rundlinge / Void in one of the round volumes

Ansicht durch den Kiefernwald von Westen / View through the pine forest from the west

Casino und Bürorundlinge am See / Restaurant and round office volumes on the lake

Landesgirokasse, Areal Reithalle Wettbewerbsentwurf
Stuttgart, 1988
Projekt

Dieser Entwurf für die Hauptverwaltung der damaligen Landesgirokasse Stuttgart auf einem Grundstück beim Hoppenlau-Friedhof gewann den ersten Preis im Wettbewerb, erwies sich jedoch als zu umstritten, um eine Planungsgenehmigung zu erhalten, da Stuttgart eine Stadt fast ohne Bürohochhäuser ist. Behnisch & Partner bauten schließlich ein niedrigeres Gebäude für die Bank auf einem anderen Grundstück (s. folgende Seiten). Das frühere Projekt ist hier wegen des unkonventionellen Ansatzes für diesen Bautyp aufgenommen worden. Bürohochhäuser sind in den meisten Fällen an der Basis breit und oben schmaler, die Geschosse eintönig, und die Bemühungen der Architekten beschränken sich auf ein imagebetontes Erscheinungsbild. Behnisch & Partner entwarfen statt dessen ein dem Baugelände entsprechendes niedriges Gebäude, aus dem das hohe erwächst. Dieses wechselt im Aufsteigen mehrfach seinen Charakter, denn die Architekten suchten die verschiedenen Abteilungen der Bank durch Blocks in unterschiedlichen Formen auszudrücken, während sie im Innern die Erschließungsräume variierten, um eine Differenzierung der Ebenen zu erreichen. Nur die sieben obersten Geschosse sind in einer einfachen rechteckigen Scheibe untergebracht, und diese wird aufgelockert durch die schräggestellten Aufzugs- und Treppenschächte, die auch die Kernstruktur bilden. Eine dreigeschossige Lücke hebt diesen Bauteil ab und bietet offene Terrassen, während der runde Block mit den Geschossen 4 bis 6 ein spektakuläres, verglastes Atrium einschließt. Das endgültige Erscheinungsbild war nicht im voraus festgelegt, sondern hätte sich im Verlauf des Entwurfsprozesses entwickeln können.

State Clearing Bank of Baden-Württemberg, competition design
Stuttgart, 1988
Project

This design for the headquarters of the State Clearing Bank on a site next to the Hoppenlau cemetery won first prize in the competition but proved too controversial to gain planning permission, since Stuttgart is a city almost without office towers. Behnisch & Partners eventually built another lower building for the bank on a different site (following pages): the earlier project is included here because of the fresh approach to the building type. Mostly, tall office blocks are wide at the base and narrower above, the floors mercilessly repetitive, and architectural effort goes into the development of an image independent of content. Instead, Behnisch & Partners made a low building responding to the site, out of which the high one grows. It changes character several times as it rises, for they sought to articulate the departments of the bank with blocks of different shapes while varying the access spaces internally to differentiate the levels. Only the top seven storeys are a simple rectangular slab, and this is relieved by angled lift and stair shafts which also form the core structure. A three-storey gap detaches this element and provides open terraces, while the ring block dominating floors 4–6 encompasses a dramatic glazed atrium. New structural possibilities opened up by computer calculation were exploited, and the final image was not preconceived, but rather allowed to develop through the design process.

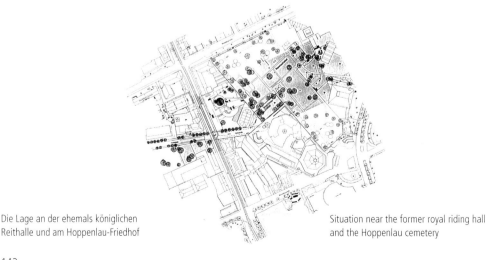

Die Lage an der ehemals königlichen Reithalle und am Hoppenlau-Friedhof

Situation near the former royal riding hall and the Hoppenlau cemetery

Verschieden ausgeformte Grundrisse im Turmbereich
Differently organised plans in the tower area

Modellansicht
Model view

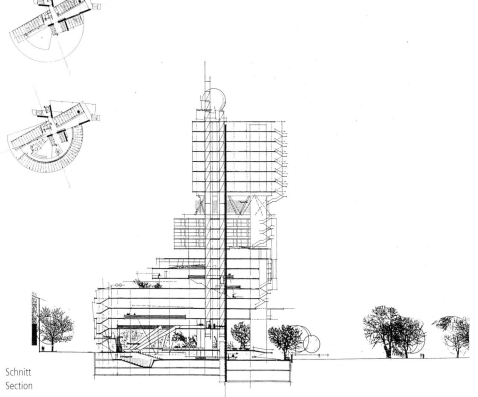

Schnitt
Section

Landesgirokasse am Bollwerk
jetzt Landesbank Baden-Württemberg
Stuttgart, 1997

Als sich zeigte, daß das Hochhaus aus dem Wettbewerb von 1988 (s. vorhergehende Seiten) nicht gebaut werden konnte, entschied die Bank sich für ein konventionelleres Bauwerk auf einem anderen Grundstück. Den neu ausgelobten Wettbewerb gewannen wiederum Behnisch & Partner. Das neue Dienstleistungsgebäude vereinigt mehrere Abteilungen auf einem innerstädtischen Grundstück mit der Bezeichnung «Bollwerk», weil es einst Teil der Befestigungsanlagen Stuttgarts war. Die Blockrandbebauung variiert von fünf bis zu acht Geschossen und beläßt die Mitte zur Belichtung und Aussicht frei. Das der Öffentlichkeit zugewandte Erdgeschoß ist anderen kommerziellen Nutzungen vorbehalten. Die Bürogeschosse darüber sind zweibündig mit nach innen und außen orientierten Arbeitsplätzen. Die vertikalen Verkehrswege sind an den Ecken plaziert; Einförmigkeit wird soweit irgend möglich vermieden. Ausblicke über die Dächer zu den umgebenden Hügeln werden durch großzügige Verglasungen und Dachterrassen ermöglicht, besonders aus dem im obersten Geschoß vorspringenden Glasriegel, der die Empfangssuite enthält. Der zentrale Innen- und Lichthof führt bis ins Untergeschoß und belichtet alle nach innen orientierten Räume. Er enthält einen Aufenthaltsbereich im Freien für die Cafeteria im Untergeschoß und ein spiegelndes Wasserbecken. Auf der linken Seite liegt die mehrgeschossige Eingangshalle unter einer großen, geneigten Glasfläche – das spektakulärste Element des gesamten Projekts. Man hat den Eindruck, als wären die Verkehrsgänge im Erd- und ersten Obergeschoß offen belassen, um sich mit dem Innenhof zu vereinigen, der dann in letzter Minute wetterfest gemacht wurde. Das Glas taucht sogar in das Becken ein und trennt die äußere Wasserfläche von einem weiteren verglasten innenliegenden Wasserbehälter.

State Clearing Bank of Baden-Württemberg
now State Bank of Baden-Württemberg
Stuttgart, 1997

When it proved impossible to build the tower resulting from the competition of 1988 (previous pages), the State Clearing Bank settled on a more conventional building and a new site. They held a new competition which was again won by Behnisch & Partners. The new headquarters brings together departments for share-dealing, foreign exchange, investment risk, property, public relations, and general administration, at a city-centre site called Bollwerk (bulwark), once part of Stuttgart's fortifications. The perimeter of the block varies from five to eight storeys, leaving the centre open for light and view. At ground level the public face is given to other uses, including a corner restaurant, a three-auditorium cinema and a designer lamp shop. Office floors above are double-loaded, the rooms looking inward and outward. Vertical circulation stacks occur near corners, and every effort is made to avoid uniformity. Views across rooftops to surrounding hills are exploited with large windows and roof-terraces, and especially in the cantilevered sky-box containing the entertainment suite. The central court and light-well extends to basement level, admitting light around the inner perimeter. It contains the outdoor sitting area for the basement cafeteria and a reflective pool. On its left side is the multi-level entrance hall set under a great sloping plane of glass, the most dramatic invention in the whole design. It is as if ground and first floor circulation galleries were left open to participate in the court then weather proofed at the last minute. The glass even plunges into the pool, dividing the main external water sheet from another glass-walled internal tank.

Die Lage des Gebäudes in bezug
zur Stadtentwicklung
Building site in relation
to the city's development

Ansicht Fritz-Elsas-Straße mit Eingangsbereich / View of Fritz-Elsas Strasse with entrance area

Innenhof. Ansicht von südlicher Ecke nach Norden / Courtyard. View from southern corner looking north

Grundriß 3. Obergeschoß
Third floor plan

Grundriß Eingangsgeschoß
Entrance floor plan

Schnitt
Section

Grundriß Untergeschoß
Lower level plan

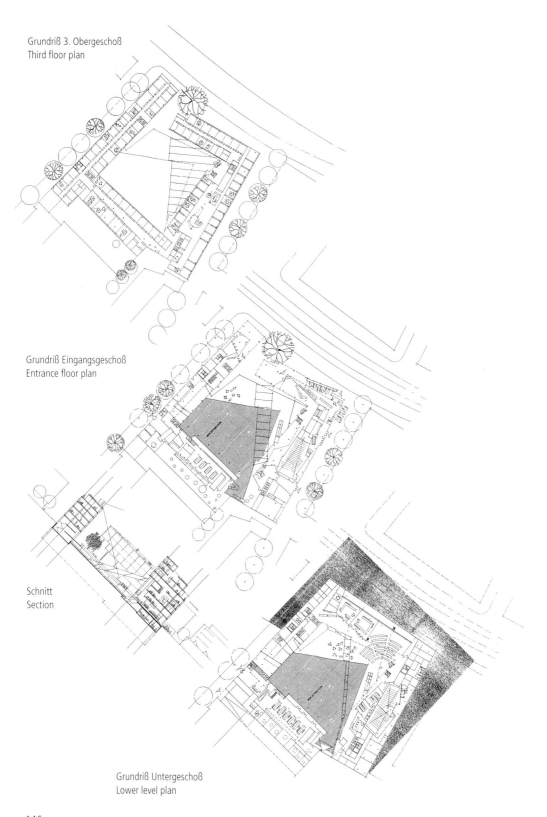

Blick durch die Schrägverglasung der Halle in den Innenhof / View of the courtyard through the foyer's angled glazing

Untergeschoß der Halle / Lower level of foyer

Blick über den See auf das Handelszentrum / View of the trade centre across the lake

Lufträume im Bürobereich / Open spaces in office area

Landesversicherungsanstalt Schleswig-Holstein
Lübeck, 1997

Ein Grundstück am Stadtrand wurde für dieses große Bürogebäude gewählt, das die widersprüchlichen Aufgaben erfüllen mußte, sich in die Nachbarbebauung einzufügen und zugleich eine eigene Identität zu entwickeln. Behnisch, Behnisch & Partner reagierten darauf mit einem niedrigen, stark gegliederten Bauwerk in einem Park, das sich sanft im Gelände und den Gärten der Umgebung auflöst. Die Büros sind in bis zu fünf Geschosse hohen Doppeltrakten untergebracht, die sternförmig in die Ecken des Grundstücks ragen und schöne Ausblicke sowie natürliche Belüftung ermöglichen. Die längsten Flure verjüngen sich mit Abnahme des Verkehrs und lenken ihn somit in die entsprechenden Richtungen. Alle Flure enden offen und sind durch vereinzelte Teeküchen aufgelockert. Sämtliche Bürotrakte führen zu einer eindrucksvollen zentralen Halle, in der die verschiedenen Ebenen durch eine Vielzahl sich überschneidender Treppen miteinander verbunden und optisch in einem großen Luftraum unter dem verglasten Dach vereint sind. Auf Erdgeschoßniveau liegen der Haupteingang und der Verteiler, die Cafeteria sowie weitere sich anschließende Gemeinschaftseinrichtungen. Die Erschließung erfolgt von Süden zwischen dem südlichen und dem östlichen Trakt, der Zugang über eine Brücke über einem Regenwasser-Rückhaltebecken. Der Vorteil der sternförmigen Anlage liegt darin, daß meist nur zwei der sechs Flügel sichtbar sind und die Masse dadurch optisch reduziert wird. Die visuelle Beziehung des Gebäudes zur umgebenden Grünfläche ist von großer Bedeutung.

Headquarters of State Insurance in Schleswig-Holstein
Lübeck, 1997

An edge of city site had been chosen for this large office building, imposing the contradictory duties of respecting the neighbourhood while creating a presence of its own. Behnisch, Behnisch & Partners responded with a low, fragmented building set in a park, which dissolves gently into surrounding allotments and gardens. The offices occupy double-loaded wings up to five-storeys high which project starfish-like into the corners of the site, enjoying good views and natural ventilation. The longest corridors taper with reducing traffic to give a sense of direction, and all are relieved with windows and occasional tea-brewing areas. All office wings lead to a dramatic central hall where levels are linked by a cascade of stairs, and joined visually in a great void under a glazed roof. At ground floor is the main entrance and distribution point, with cafeteria and other communal facilities adjacent. The approach is from the south, between south and east wings, the drive arriving across a bridge over an ornamental lake. The advantage of the starfish plan is that for most of the time only two of the six wings are visible, reducing the apparent bulk. Much depends on the visual relationship of building and surrounding garden.

Die Lage des Gebäudes westlich der Altstadt
Building site west of the old town

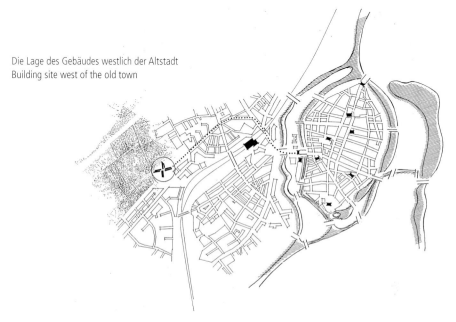

Grundriß Erdgeschoß
Ground floor plan

Grundriß Untergeschoß mit dem Speisesaal
Plan of lower level with dining room

Schnitt durch die Halle
Section through hall

Ansicht von der Autobahn / View from the motorway

Eingangsbereich mit Halle / Entrance area with hall

Ansicht der Eingangshalle / View of entrance hall

Die neue Hauptverwaltung am See / The new headquarters on the lake

Eröffnungsfeierlichkeiten in der Halle
Opening celebrations in the hall

Blick vom Dach in die Halle
View from the roof into the hall

Einer der Lufträume in den Büroflügeln mit Verbindungstreppen
One of the open spaces in the office wings with connecting staircases

Der Speisesaal mit «Lichtwolke» / Dining area with "Cloud of Light"

Verwaltungs- und Ausstellungsgebäude der Firma VS – Vereinigte Spezialmöbelfabriken
Tauberbischofsheim, 1998

Der über hundert Jahre alte Familienbetrieb entstand als Produktionsstätte von Spezialmöbeln für Schulen, erweiterte das Programm jedoch auf Büromöbel und stellt ein Möbelsystem nach dem Entwurf von Behnisch & Partner mit Hubert Eilers her. Das neue Gebäude sollte die auf verschiedene Häuser verteilten Büros vereinen sowie Ausstellungsbereiche, Konferenz- und Empfangsräume für Besucher und ein Mitarbeiterrestaurant enthalten. Behnisch, Behnisch & Partner planten einen 110 m langen, fünfgeschossigen Block, der das ansteigende Gelände nutzt und zwei Altbauten miteinander verbindet. Der Haupteingang von Osten führt von einer öffentlichen Straße in eine zweigeschossige, verglaste Halle, die einladend neben das Restaurant gesetzt ist. Eine Treppenflucht verbindet direkt alle Ebenen. Die Zwischengeschosse dienen als Ausstellungsflächen für Firmenprodukte, während die beiden obersten Geschosse zweibündige Büroräume enthalten. Die Nordfassade ist zum neu entstandenen grünen Hof im Zentrum der Anlage orientiert; ein bestehender Feuerlöschteich wurde architektonisch genutzt, als ob er unter dem Gebäude hindurchfließt. Im Gegensatz dazu ist die aufgelöste Fassade zu einem Wohnquartier gerichtet; sie ist in Terrassen abgestuft, um das Sonnenlicht besser zu nutzen. Die Architektur ist heiter und modern, teilweise transparent und auch stark farbig. Sie soll die Gestaltphilosophie der Firma wiedergeben.

Offices and exhibition space for the VS – Furniture Factory
Tauberbischofsheim, 1998

The century-old family firm grew up as a producer of specialist furniture for schools but diversified into office furniture, even commissioning a desk system design from Behnisch & Partners in collaboration with Hubert Eilers. The task of their new building was to unite offices dispersed across the site, to provide exhibition, conference and reception spaces for customers, and a new staff restaurant. Behnisch, Behnisch & Partners responded with an 110 m five storey block, using rising ground and linking two existing buildings. The east-facing main entrance comes off the public street into a two-storey glazed hall placed invitingly close to the restaurant. A running stair links directly to all levels. The intermediate floors offer exhibition spaces both for historic furniture and current products, while the two top floors contain double-loaded offices. The north facade fronts the newly formed green court at the heart of the works, an existing fire pond being exploited for architectural effect by seeming to flow under the building. In contrast, the informal south facade gently overlooks a residential quarter, stepping back progressively in terraces to enjoy the sun. The architecture is briskly modern, in places transparent but also highly coloured. It was intended to reflect the design aspirations of the firm.

Restaurant und Casino / Restaurant

Zugangsbereich von Nord-Osten
Entrance area seen from the north-east

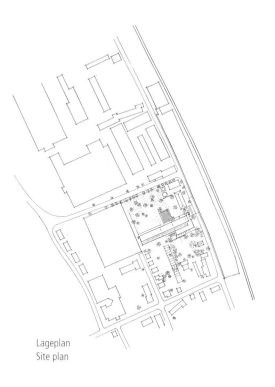

Lageplan
Site plan

Ansicht von Süden / View from the south

Ausstellungsbereich / Exhibition area

Ansicht von Nord-Westen / View from the north-west

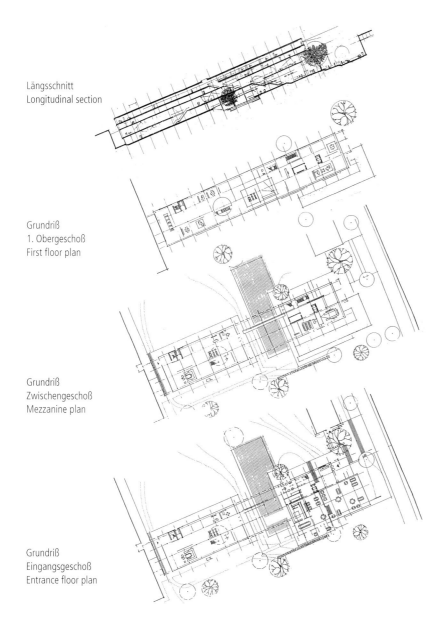

Längsschnitt
Longitudinal section

Grundriß
1. Obergeschoß
First floor plan

Grundriß
Zwischengeschoß
Mezzanine plan

Grundriß
Eingangsgeschoß
Entrance floor plan

Verkehrsbauten

Fußgängerbereich Königstraße/Schloßplatz und U-Bahn-Station
Stuttgart, 1980

Die Umgestaltung von Schloßplatz und Königstraße im Herzen Stuttgarts ist eine der größten, aber am wenigsten sichtbaren Arbeiten des Büros Behnisch & Partner. Die Entscheidung, diese Straßenachse in eine Fußgängerzone umzuwandeln, und die Maßnahmen zu ihrer Umgestaltung haben großen Einfluß auf die Gestaltung des Stadtzentrums ausgeübt und eine neue Atmosphäre geschaffen. Dennoch bestand keine Chance für einen Neubau, und es war weder notwendig noch wünschenswert, eine durchgehende architektonische Handschrift zu zeigen. Die Architekten leisteten große Arbeit: Sie mußten alle notwendigen Anlieferungswege planen, die Enden der Fußgängerzone gestalten und sie mit den Anliegerstraßen verbinden, die Landschafts- und Bodengestaltung, darunter auch Niveauverschiebungen, durchführen und Straßenmöblierung, Bänke und Schutzdächer einfügen. Sie wurden sogar aufgefordert, die Unterführungen und U-Bahn-Stationen aufzuwerten, obgleich die schweren Konstruktionen bereits von Ingenieuren geplant worden waren. Um den Beitrag von Behnisch & Partnern angemessen zu beurteilen, wäre es notwendig, den früheren Zustand des Bereiches mit dem jetzigen zu vergleichen. Daß er von den Stadtbewohnern angenommen wird, ist ein großes Kompliment.

Buildings for Transport

Pedestrian zone and underground station
Central Stuttgart, 1980

The reworking of Schlossplatz and Königstrasse at the heart of Stuttgart is one of Behnisch & Partners' largest but least visible works. The decision to pedestrianise this spinal street and the measures taken to reorganise it have been hugely influential in shaping the city centre and creating a new atmosphere, yet there was no chance to make a distinct building, and it was neither necessary nor desirable to impose a consistent architectural signature. The architects did much work: they had to plan all necessary service routes, to deal with the ends of the pedestrian zone and its connection to adjacent streets, to decide the landscaping and ground treatment including changes of level, and to add street-furniture, seats and shelters. They were even asked to deck out the interiors of the subways and underground stations, though the heavy structures had already been designed by engineers. Properly to appreciate their contribution, it would be necessary to compare the area as it was before the change took place with the way it is now. That it is taken for granted by citizens is a great compliment.

Lichtflecken unter dem Blätterdach der Platanen / Patches of light beneath the plane trees' leafy roof

Glasschirme
Glass umbrellas

«Pusteblumenbrunnen»
"Dandelion fountain"

Die Königstraße vom Bahnhofsturm
Königstrasse from the tower of the railway station

Lageplan / Site plan

Aufsicht auf den Schloßplatz vom Marquardtbau / View of Schlossplatz from the Marquardt building

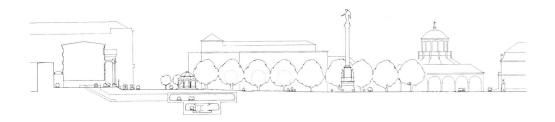

Schnitt durch den Schloßplatz / Section through Schlossplatz

Bahnsteig
Platform

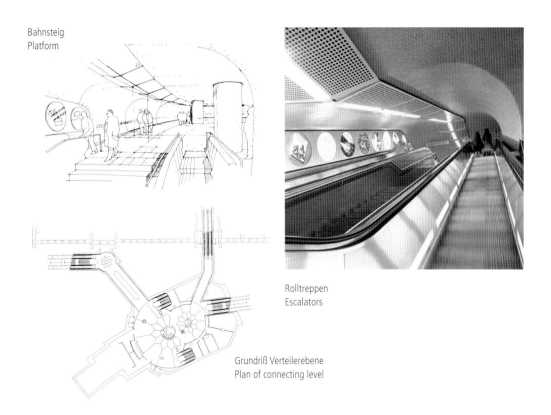

Rolltreppen
Escalators

Grundriß Verteilerebene
Plan of connecting level

Die Verteilerebene unter dem Schloßplatz / Connecting level beneath Schlossplatz

161

Umgestaltung des Wiener Platzes
Stuttgart-Feuerbach, 1991

Remodelling of Wiener Platz
Stuttgart-Feuerbach, 1991

Feuerbach war früher ein eigenständiger Ort, wurde jedoch im Verlauf des Wachstums der Stadt Stuttgart eingemeindet und in das städtische Verkehrssystem eingebunden, wodurch der kreisförmige, aus dem 19. Jahrhundert stammende Wiener Platz weitgehend zerstört wurde. Zuerst trennte die erhöht geführte S-Bahn den Bereich, und der Bahnhof übernahm eine beherrschende Rolle; dann verlor der alte Kreis zusätzlich sein Gesicht durch einen Fabrikbau, der eine der Zufahrtsstraßen blockiert. Im Krieg wurde ein Bunker in Form eines kegelförmigen Betonturms gebaut. Straßen- und Stadtbahn kamen hinzu, kreuzen vor dem Bahnhofsgebäude und verschwinden dann rasch im Untergrund. Die Zubringer von der Autobahn führten zu einem Einbahnstraßensystem um sechs Blocks herum; zu einer seiner Einmündungen wurden die Reste des Wiener Platzes. Behnisch & Partner suchten diese Anhäufung kollidierender Elemente aufzulösen, indem sie neue Straßen- und Stadtbahn-Stationen, eine Bus-Station und eine Fußgängerunterführung planten. Nachdem sie vergeblich versucht hatten, einen einheitlichen Plan durchzusetzen, erkannten sie, daß zu viele widerstreitende Interessen am Werk waren, als daß eine saubere, einfache Lösung zu erreichen gewesen wäre. Statt dessen entschieden sie sich für ein «collageähnliches» Vorgehen, bei dem die Stadtbahn- und die Bus-Station jeweils eine selbständige Identität erhielten. Der Bunker wurde durch hinzugefügte frei geformte Glasdächer in ein plastisches Objekt verwandelt, während die Stadtbahn-Station mit leichten, farbigen Überdachungen versehen wurde, die durch ihre Größe und Raffinesse eine überraschende Präsenz entwickeln. Mit wenigen, aber durchdachten Gesten wurde der Platz in einen einprägsamen Ort verwandelt. Er ist kein städtisches Zentrum, kein Marktplatz, vielmehr ein Verbindungselement dort, wo die Dinge aufeinandertreffen und wieder auseinandergehen.

Feuerbach was once an independent place, but as the outer suburbs grew it was taken over by transport links, and the circular 19th century Wienerplatz was largely obliterated. First the raised S-Bahn divided the space, its station taking a dominant role, then the old circus was further weakened by a factory blocking one of its streets. The war brought a bomb shelter with conical concrete tower, and thereafter a bus station to connect with the railway. The tram and underground system arrived, crossing in front of the station then quickly disappearing into the earth. Feeder roads from the autobahn prompted a one-way system circling six blocks, the remains of Wiener Platz becoming one of its junctions. Behnisch & Partners sought to resolve this accumulation of conflicting elements while providing new tram and underground stations, a bus station, and a pedestrian underpass. After struggling to develop a unified master plan, they realised that too many conflicting interests were at work for any kind of neat, simple solution to be imposed. Instead they resorted to a 'collage-like' approach, allowing tram station, bus station and underpass to develop independent identities. Transformed into a sculptural object, the bunker was given a lively skirt of glazed roofs, while the tram station received lightweight coloured canopies which have a surprising presence for their size and delicacy. With a few careful gestures the space was transformed into a memorable place. It is no urban focus, no market square, but rather a link-place where things for a moment come together only to disperse again.

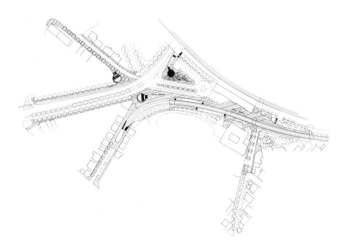

Lageplan Wiener Platz
Site plan of Wiener Platz

Untersicht der Überdachung der Bushaltestelle / Underside view of bus station roof

Der Bunker mit den neuen Dachflügeln / Bunker with new roof wings

Überdachung der Stadtbahnstation / Roof of municipal train station

Tunnelmund der
Fußgängerunterführung
Tunnel entrance of the
pedestrian underpass

Flughafenkontrollturm
Nürnberg, 1998

Als Nürnberg noch im Grenzbereich zur DDR lag, war sein Flughafen von geringer Bedeutung. Die Wiedervereinigung führte eine Erweiterung als regionales Bindeglied mit sich, so daß die Zunahme des Verkehrs einen neuen Kontrollturm erforderte. Er steht in einer Gebäudereihe auf der Südseite des Rollfelds zwischen einem bestehenden und einem größeren geplanten Hangar. Das Hauptelement der plastischen Komposition ist der Turm für die Fluglotsen, der sich für eine unbehinderte Rundumsicht 45 m über Geländehöhe erhebt. Seine Betonkonstruktion ist vorgeneigt, so daß die sechzehneckige Glaskanzel aus der vorhandenen Hallenflucht herausragt. Das horizontale Hauptelement ist ein nach Osten orientierter Trakt mit aneinandergereihten Büroräumen, der auf Stützen steht und in den Grünraum hineinragt. Westlich davon ist in einem kürzeren und geschlosseneren Trakt die technische Ausstattung untergebracht, und zwischen beiden breitet sich eine verglaste Eingangshalle aus. Der Zugang erfolgt durch eine zweigeschossige Glaswand am Ende der Halle. Direkt auf der Westseite unter die Kanzel gehängt ist ein containerähnliches Betriebselement, das die Flugsicherungsgeräte und die Klimaanlage enthält. Darunter ist der Aufenthaltsraum der Mitarbeiter mit einer offenen Terrasse und eigenem Dach auf die eingeschossigen Bauteile gesetzt.

Airport control tower
Nuremberg, 1998

When it lay next to the border with East Germany, Nuremberg Airport was of marginal importance, but reunification brought expansion as a regional link, and increasing traffic demanded a new control tower. It joins a row of buildings on the south side of the airfield, set between an existing hangar and a larger planned one. The main vertical element is the tower for air-traffic controllers, raised 45 m above ground level for a clear allround view. Its concrete structure is canted forward, projecting the sixteen-sided control room out over the building line. The main horizontal element is a single-loaded east-facing office wing elevated on columns and running right back into the site. To west a shorter and solider wing contains technical services, and a generous glazed entrance hall develops between the two. Entry is through a two-storey glass wall at the end of the hall. Slung just beneath the control room on the west side is a container-like servicing element containing air traffic control equipment and air-conditioning plant. Directly beneath, topping the ground-level buildings with its own separate roof and external balcony, is the staff recreation area.

Schnitt durch die Kanzel
Section through control room

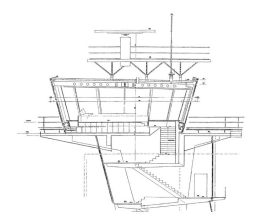

Kanzel für die Fluglotsen / Traffic control room

Ansicht von Nord-Westen / View from north-west

Grundriß 1. Obergeschoß
First floor plan

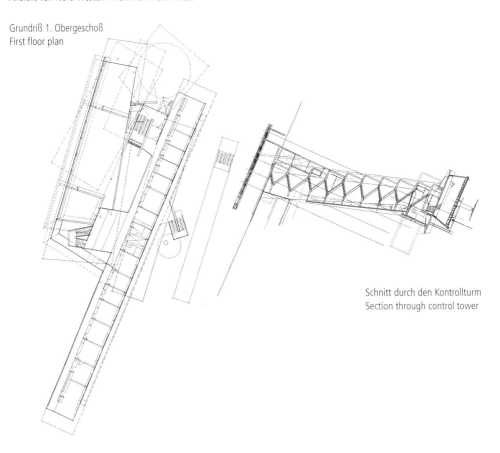

Schnitt durch den Kontrollturm
Section through control tower

Eingangshalle mit Galerieebene / Entrance hall with gallery level

Blick durch die Oberlichtverglasung der Halle auf den Turm
View of tower through the hall's skylight glazing

Bundesbauten

Bundesbauten und ihre Integration in die Stadt Bonn
Wettbewerb und Weiterbearbeitungen
Bonn, 1973 – 1975

Als Deutschland nach dem Zweiten Weltkrieg geteilt worden war, entschied man sich für Bonn als Regierungssitz. Eine moderne Schule am Ufer des Rheins wurde zum Plenarbereich umgebaut und von Hans Schwippert ein neuer Parlamentssaal angebaut. Im Jahre 1972, auf dem Höhepunkt des wirtschaftlichen Booms, erwog die deutsche Regierung den Ersatz dieses «Provisoriums» durch einen völlig neuen Komplex für Bundestag und Bundesrat mit zugehörigen Büros sowie Räumen für die Ausschüsse. Ein Wettbewerb wurde ausgeschrieben, in dem Behnisch & Partner einen der vier ersten Preise erhielten. In diesem ersten, 1973/75 erarbeiteten Entwurf breitete sich ein Komplex mit mehreren Zentren in einer parkähnlichen Landschaft aus und erreichte seinen Höhepunkt im kreisförmigen Bundestag. Die ringförmig angeordneten Bürogebäude brachen den Maßstab der Gesamtanlage in vernünftige Dimensionen auf und boten eine saubere Lösung des Problems, alle diese Räume mit Tageslicht, Ausblick und zu öffnenden Fenstern zu versorgen bei Entfernungen von maximal fünf Minuten Fußweg zum Parlamentssaal. Der Komplex war wohl auf Egon Eiermanns Abgeordneten-Hochhaus «Langer Eugen» konzentriert, die Außenräume waren als Landschaft behandelt, die um die Gebäude herum und unter ihnen hindurchlief.

Political Buildings

New Parliament buildings
preliminary designs
Bonn, 1973 – 1975

When Germany was divided after the war, Bonn was chosen as the seat of government. A Modernist school on the bank of the Rhine was converted for parliamentary use, extended with a new parliamentary chamber by Schwippert. In 1972, at the height of the economic boom, the German Government considered replacing this 'provisional' arrangement with a whole new complex comprising Bundestag and Bundesrat along with necessary offices and committee rooms. They held a competition, and Behnisch & Partners was one of four first-prize winners. In their initial plan, developed in 1973/75, a multi-centred complex sprawled across a park-like landscape, reaching a climax in a circular Bundestag. The ring-shaped office buildings broke down the scale of the whole to reasonable dimensions, neatly solving the problem of giving everyone daylight, view and openable windows, while keeping them within five minutes walk of the parliamentary chamber. The complex would have focused well on Eiermann's 'Big Eugen' office tower, but the landscape was treated somewhat residually as a park that flowed around and under the buildings.

Bundesbauten in Bonn. Gesamtmodell Realisierungswettbewerb 1973
Federal buildings in Bonn. General model, competition 1973

Zweite Stufe für die Planung der Bundesbauten in Bonn 1974/1975. Blick in eine der Hallen
Second phase for the design of the Federal buildings in Bonn 1974/1975. View into one of the open spaces

Ansicht vom Rhein / View from the Rhine

Wettbewerbsentwurf 1973, Detailmodell / Competition design 1973, Detail model

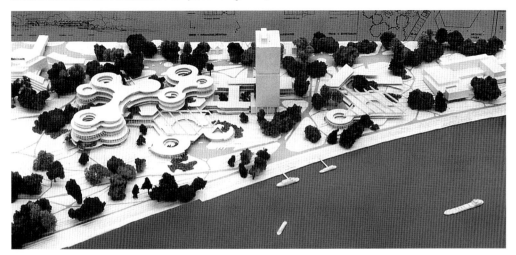

«Grüne Mitte»
Bonn, 1979

Die Gedanken entwickelten sich weiter, und nach langen Diskussionen wurde 1979 ein neuer Generalplan vorgelegt, bei dem die Betonung auf einer Grünfläche als Parlamentsbereich lag. Ein öffentlicher Park zwischen Schnellstraße und Rhein sollte von den Gebäuden der verschiedenen Organe der Demokratie umgeben werden – von den beiden Parlamenten, den Büros, den Bauten für den Bundespräsidenten und für die Ländervertretungen. Dieser zentrale Bereich sollte als Arena für Begegnungen dem Volk gehören, der befestigte Bereich vor dem Bundestag zum offiziellen Parlamentsplatz werden. Der Entwurf war weit fortgeschritten, als die Ölkrise eintrat und die vor den mutmaßlichen Kosten für den Steuerzahler zurückschreckenden Politiker beschlossen, ihre großartigen Planungen ad acta zu legen und weiterhin die vorhandenen Parlamentsbauten zu nutzen. Dies führte zu Behnischs endgültigem Entwurf, der auf den folgenden Seiten wiedergegeben ist.

"Green Centre"
Bonn, 1979

The ideas were developed and after much discussion a new general plan submitted in 1979, in which the emphasis was on a "Green Centre" for the parliamentary zone. A public park between main road and Rhine, this was to be surrounded by the various organs of democracy – the two parliamentary chambers, offices, buildings for the Federal President and for the various Länder. This focal point would belong to the people, an arena for meetings, the paved area outside the Bundestag becoming the official parliamentary square. The idea was well-advanced when the oil crisis struck, and the politicians, already embarrassed at the proposed cost to the taxpayer, decided to shelve their grandiose plans, keeping the existing parliament buildings. This led to the final Behnisch scheme, which is presented opposite.

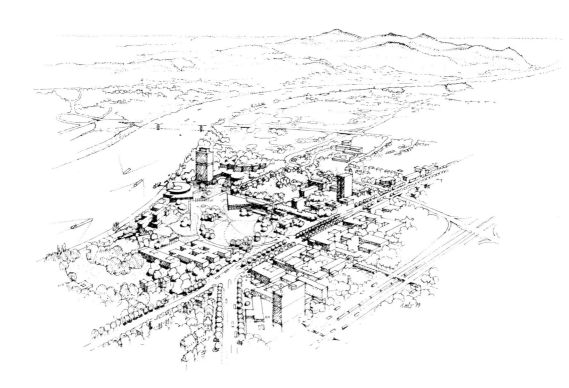

Bundesbauten in Bonn mit «Grüner Mitte». Zeichnung: Carlo Weber
Federal buildings in Bonn with "Green Centre". Drawing: Carlo Weber

Plenarbereich des Deutschen Bundestags
Bonn, 1983–1992

Behnisch & Partner wurde zunächst die Aufgabe übertragen, einen neuen Eingangsbereich für den bestehenden Plenarsaal zu entwerfen. Später wurde der Auftrag erweitert um den Neubau des Plenarsaals an der Stelle des alten, das Restaurant für die Abgeordneten und den Präsidialbereich. Diese Elemente wurden behutsam in die Rheinaue zwischen die bestehenden Bauten eingefügt. Aufgrund deren asymmetrischer Position konnte der Eingang nicht auf die gleiche Achse mit dem Parlamentsgebäude gestellt werden. Die daraus folgende seitliche Verschiebung ist vor allem an der Haupttreppe sichtbar, die auch entgegen der Erwartung abwärts führt, da der Weg für die Parlamentarier zum Rhein abfällt. Dagegen verläuft der Zugang für das Publikum zur Galerie eben. Der Plenarsaal ist kreisförmig angelegt, um die Gleichberechtigung aller Volksvertreter zu betonen. Die politischen Parteien nehmen die Abschnitte von links nach rechts ein, und es gibt, anders als im alten Reichstag, keine klare räumliche Trennung zwischen Regierung und Opposition oder Abgeordneten und Ministern. Im Gegensatz zur Kreisform des Saales sind die Galerien für Publikum und Presse auf der oberen Ebene orthogonal angeordnet, um sie vom politischen Geschehen zu trennen. Das ganze Gebäude ist gemäß der Vorstellung von einer transparenten Regierungsform verglast und der Rhein als Nord-Süd-Achse des Landes und historisch bedeutsame Wasserstraße sichtbar. Eine große, runde Öffnung in der Decke mit ausgeklügeltem Lichtlenksystem erfüllt den Plenarsaal mit Tageslicht. Die rhythmisch gegliederten Fassaden mit Elementen aus Glas und Stahl wiederholen in weiterentwickelter Form die rationalistische Sprache Mies van der Rohes und seiner im Nachkriegsdeutschland wirkenden Nachfolger Sep Ruf und Egon Eiermann, die beide auf dem Regierungsgelände gebaut haben. Das Innere ist lebendig und asymmetrisch mit fließenden Raumfolgen und sich optisch durchdringenden Ebenen. Der lange, niedrige Raum des Restaurants wurde durch die Mitwirkung des Künstlers Nicola de Maria zu einem besonderen Höhepunkt.

Parliament building
Bonn, 1983–1992

At first, Behnisch & Partners were asked only to create a new entrance and foyer for the existing parliamentary chamber, but later the task was extended to include a replacement Chamber, a new restaurant for members, and a block of offices for the Parliamentary President (equivalent to the UK Speaker). These elements were placed carefully between the existing buildings, whose asymmetrical positions forced the entrance out of alignment with the axis of the chamber. The consequent sideways shift is most visible in the main stair, which also unexpectedly runs in a downward direction, since the members' path sinks with the falling ground towards the Rhine. Meanwhile, the public's route to their gallery runs through at the same level. The chamber is based on a circular principle to stress equality, since all members represent the people. The political parties occupy segments from left to right, and unlike the old Reichstag, there is no clear spatial distinction between government and opposition, or members and ministers. In contrast with the circle, the galleries for public and press at the upper level take a rectangular form to detach them from the political process. The whole building is glazed in sympathy with the idea of open government, and to make the Rhine visible both as the north-south axis of the nation, and as a historic route. A sophisticated roof lighting system bathes the chamber in daylight, controlling exposure with motorised louvres. Steel and glass facades with rhythmic elements reiterate in developed form the rationalist language of Mies and German followers such as Sep Ruf and Egon Eiermann, both of whom contributed earlier buildings to the government complex. The interiors are lively and irregular, with flowing spaces and visually interacting layers appropriate to the 1990s. The long low space of the restaurant, which Behnisch considered a potential problem, was completely transformed by a vibrant colour scheme from the artist Nicola de Maria.

Die realisierte Anlage in der Rheinaue
The realised ensemble in the Rheinaue environment
Zeichnung / drawing: Gerald Staib

Parlamentsplatz mit Skulptur von Olaf Metzel
Parliament square with sculpture by Olaf Metzel

Eingangshalle der ehemaligen Pädagogischen Akademie aus dem Jahr 1932
Entrance hall and former Academy of Education from 1932

Übergangszonen vom Verbindungsteil zum Südflügel / Transitional areas between connecting building to south wing

Lageplan
Site plan

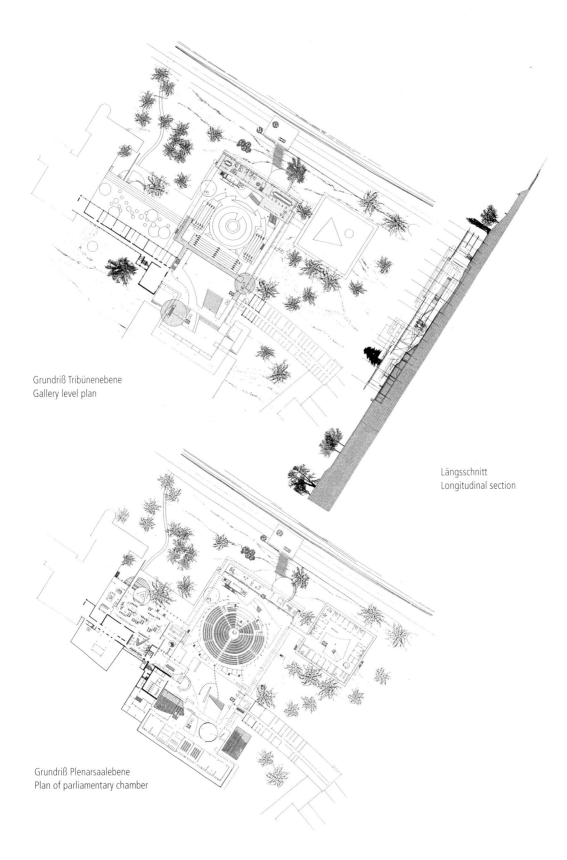

Grundriß Tribünenebene
Gallery level plan

Längsschnitt
Longitudinal section

Grundriß Plenarsaalebene
Plan of parliamentary chamber

Eingangshalle und Lobby mit
großer Treppe
Entrance hall with lobby and
main stair

Freie Lichtlinien
Free lines of light

Vogelnesttreppe und Blick in den Plenarsaal / Bird's nest stair and view into the parliamentary chamber

Die kreisrunde Sitzordnung im Plenarsaal / The circular seating order in the parliamentary chamber
Handskizze / Free-hand sketch: Günter Behnisch

Untersicht Lichtdach
Bottom view of light roof

Blick von der Besuchertribüne in den Plenarsaal / View from the public gallery into the parliamentary chamber

Halle im Präsidialbereich / Hall in the presidential area

Der Plenar- und Präsidialbereich am Rhein. Skulptur von Mark di Suvero
The parliamentary and presidential areas on the Rhine. Sculpture by Mark di Suvero

Bundestagsrestaurant mit Decken- und Wandmalereien von Nicola de Maria
Parliamentary restaurant with ceiling and wall paintings of Nicola de Maria

Biographien / Biographies

Günter Behnisch eröffnete sein erstes Büro in Stuttgart 1952.
Seit 1966 hat Günter Behnisch als «Behnisch & Partner» mit Partnern gearbeitet, und zwar mit Fritz Auer (bis 1979), Winfried Büxel (bis 1992), Manfred Sabatke, Erhard Tränkner (bis 1993), Carlo Weber (bis 1979), und mit Seniorarchitekt Christian Kandzia (seit 1969).
1989 eröffnete Günter Behnisch ein zweites Büro in der Innenstadt Stuttgarts in Partnerschaft mit Stefan Behnisch (seit 1992) und Günther Schaller (seit 1997), heute «Behnisch, Behnisch & Partner».
Das alte Büro «Behnisch & Partner» firmiert heute bei manchen Projekten auch als «Günter Behnisch und Manfred Sabatke». Dieses Büro hat seinen Sitz nach wie vor im Stuttgarter Vorort Sillenbuch.

Günter Behnisch opened his first office in Stuttgart in 1952.
Since 1966 Günter Behnisch has worked as "Behnisch & Partner" with partners Fritz Auer (until 1979), Winfried Büxel (until 1992), Manfred Sabatke, Erhard Tränkner (until 1993), Carlo Weber (until 1979), and with senior architect Christian Kandzia (since 1969).
In 1989 Günter Behnisch opened a second office in downtown Stuttgart in partnership with Stefan Behnisch (since 1992) and Günther Schaller (since 1997), now "Behnisch, Behnisch & Partner".
Today the old office "Behnisch & Partner" signs some projects as "Günter Behnisch und Manfred Sabatke". This office retains its location in the Stuttgart suburb of Sillenbuch.

Behnisch & Partner/
Günter Behnisch and Manfred Sabatke

Partners and senior architects:
Günter Behnisch – Manfred Sabatke – Christian Kandzia

Office address: Gorch-Fock-Straße 30, D-70 619 Stuttgart
Phone: 07 11/47 65 60, Telefax: 07 11/4 76 56 56
e-mail: bp@behnisch.com

Günter Behnisch

Born 1922	Dresden, married to Johanna Behnisch (maiden name Fink), three children
1947–1951	studies in Architecture, Technical University of Stuttgart (Dipl.-Ing.)
1951–1952	works at Prof. Rolf Gutbrod's office in Stuttgart
1952	sets up his own office
Since 1966	Behnisch & Partner
	Since 1966 Behnisch, Auer, Büxel, Sabatke (from 1970), Tränkner, Weber
	Since 1979 Behnisch, Büxel, Sabatke, Tränkner
	Now Günter Behnisch and Manfred Sabatke
1967	Professor for Design, Industrial Buildings and Planning Director of the Institute for Building Standardisation at the Technical University, Darmstadt
Since 1969	co-operation with Christian Kandzia, now senior architect
1982	member of the Akademie der Künste Berlin

1984	Honorary Doctorate, University of Stuttgart
1987	retires from University duties
From 1989	establishes city office Stuttgart, now: Behnisch, Behnisch & Partner. Günter Behnisch, Stefan Behnisch, Günther Schaller
1991	Professor of the International Academy of Architecture, Sofia
1992	Honorary Member of the Royal Incorporation of Architects in Scotland, Edinburgh
1992	Medaille d'Or, l'Académie d'Architecture, Paris
1992	Honorary Award, International Olympic Committee for Special Services in the Field of Sports and Architecture
1993	Hans-Molfenter-Award for special artistic achievements, State Capital of Stuttgart
1993	Honorary Professor, Technical University of Karlsruhe
1994	Member of the International Academy of Architecture, Sofia
1994	Honorary Award, Lithuanian Architecture Association, Vilnius
1995	Honorary Member of the Royal Institute of British Architects, London
1996	Founding Member of the Saxon Academy of Fine Arts, Dresden
1997	Order of Merit of the Federal Republic of Germany
1998	Fritz-Schumacher-Award, Alfred Toepfer Foundation, Hamburg
1999	Member of the Akademie der Künste Bayern

Manfred Sabatke

Born 1938	Pyritz/Pommern, married, three children
1957 – 1964	studies in Architecture, Technical University, Stuttgart (Dipl.-Ing.)
1964 – 1967	works at Yamasaki + Assoc., Gunnar Birkerts + Assoc. Birmingham, Michigan, USA
Since 1967	free lance architect, Behnisch & Partner
Since 1970	partner at Behnisch & Partner
Since 1982	Professor at the Technical College of Augsburg, for Design, Design Planning, Construction

Christian Kandzia

Born 1939	Breslau (now Wroclaw), two daughters
1960 – 1962	Apprenticeship in concrete construction studies at the Folkwang School for Design (Lithography, Serigraphy), Essen-Werden
1962 – 1969	studies in Architecture, Hochschule für Bildende Künste, Berlin (Dipl.-Ing.)
Since 1969	architect in Behnisch & Partner, now senior architect
1990 – 1993	lecturer in Architectural Photography, Technical College, Stuttgart
Since 1994	architectural adviser for Behnisch, Behnisch & Partner
Since 1995	International Visiting Scholar, Adjunct Faculty Member, Miami University, Department of Architecture, and School of Fine Arts, Oxford, Ohio, USA, and Miami University Luxembourg Architecture and Urban Design Studio. David B. Maxfield Lecture 1998
Since 1998	Curator of the West Saxon University for Technology and Economics, Zwickau

Behnisch, Behnisch & Partner

Partners: Günter Behnisch – Stefan Behnisch – Günther Schaller
Adviser: Christian Kandzia

Office address: Christophstraße 6, D-70 178 Stuttgart
Phone: 07 11 / 60 77 20, Telefax: 07 11 / 6 07 72 99
e-mail: buero@behnisch.com

Stefan Behnisch

Born 1957	Stuttgart, married to Petra Behnisch (maiden name Fries), two sons
1976 – 1979	studies in Philosophy, Philosophische Hochschule der Jesuiten, München

1978	Bakkalaureus Artius of Philosophy
1977 – 1979	studies in Economics, Ludwig Maximilians University, München
1979 – 1988	studies in Architecture, Technical University of Karlsruhe
1984 – 1985	works at Stephen Woolley & Associates Architects in Venice, California
Since 1987	works at Behnisch & Partner
Since 1988	management of Behnisch & Partner, Büro Innenstadt
Since 1992	principal partner, Behnisch, Behnisch & Partner. Günter Behnisch, Stefan Behnisch, Günther Schaller
1987 – 1989	lecturer, University of Stuttgart, Prof. Sulzer
Since 1990	several seminars and lectures at German and foreign universities
Since 1997	visiting design critic, University of Portsmouth
1998	seminar and lecture at 'International Week', School of Architecture, Nancy
Since 1998	visiting design critic, Bergen Architecture School

Günter Behnisch

see page 181

Günther Schaller

Born 1959	Neuhausen
1982 – 1987	studies in Architecture, Technical University of Stuttgart (Dipl.-Ing. FH)
1988 – 1991	studies in Architecture, University of Stuttgart (Dipl.-Ing.)
1986 – 1988	works at Kyncl + Arnold Architects, Zürich
1988 – 1991	works at Beyer, Weitbrecht, Wolz Architects, Stuttgart
Since 1989	free lance architect – competitions
Since 1991	architect, Behnisch & Partner Architects, Stuttgart
Since 1992	project partner, new office building of Landesgirokasse, Stuttgart
1992 – 1994	lecturer, University of Stuttgart
Since 1997	partner, Behnisch, Behnisch & Partner. Günter Behnisch, Stefan Behnisch, Günther Schaller

Zu den vorgestellten Arbeiten /
Credits for the presented buildings and projects

Hohenstaufen grammar school, Göppingen
Hohenstaufenstraße 39
Client: Stadt Göppingen
Architects: Günter Behnisch with
                   Bruno Lambart

Vogelsang school, Stuttgart
Paulusstraße 30
Client: Landeshauptstadt Stuttgart
Architects: Günter Behnisch with
                   Bruno Lambart

Ulm engineering school
Prittwitzstraße 10
Client: Land Baden-Württemberg
Architects: Günter Behnisch with
                   Bruno Lambart
Project team: Winfried Büxel,
                   Manfred Sabatke,
                   Erhard Tränkner, Carlo Weber,
                   Erich Becker
Landscape with: Günther Grzimek

Grammar school, now secondary modern school, Furtwangen
Ilbenstraße 10
Client: Stadt Furtwangen
Architects: Günter Behnisch with Lothar
                   Seidel and Carlo Weber
With: Paul Schirm

"In den Berglen" school, Oppelsbohm
Client: Nachbarschaftsschulverband
                   Oppelsbohm, Kreis Waiblingen
Architects: Behnisch & Partners
Co-worker: Arnd Friedemann

Auf dem Schäfersfeld grammar school, Lorch
Client: Stadt Lorch
Architects: Behnisch & Partners
Project architects: Hannes Hübner, Hermann Peltz
Project architect
of extension: Sabine Hammer
Site supervision: Lothar Frey, Lorch
Extension with: Architekturbüro Hermann

Fritz Erler school, Pforzheim
Westliche Karl-Friedrich-Straße 215
Client: Stadt Pforzheim
Architects: Behnisch & Partners
Project architect: Manfred Sabatke (partner)
Project team: Hermann Peltz, Jürgen Kröpsch,
                   Klaus Trojan, Kie Tjong Thio

Seminary Centre of the Württemberg Protestant Church, Stuttgart-Birkach
Grüninger Straße 25
Client: Evangelische Kirche
                   in Württemberg
Architects: Behnisch & Partners
Project team: Carlo Weber (project partner),
                   Winfried Büxel (partner)
Co-workers: Claudia Häfele, Hajo Kruse
Site architect: Rudolf Lettner
Landscape with: Hans Luz + Partner

Auf dem Schäfersfeld secondary modern school, Lorch
Client: Stadt Lorch
Architects: Behnisch & Partners
Project architect: Christian Kandzia
Co-worker: Dieter Kauffmann
Site supervison: Lothar Frey, Lorch

Albert Schweitzer special school, Bad Rappenau
Wagnerstraße 5
Client: Stadt Bad Rappenau
Architects: Behnisch & Partners
Project architect: Wolfgang Hinkfoth
Construction
supervision: Jürgen Mattmann, Werner Eberle,
                   Martin Hühn
Landscape with: Hans Luz + Partner

Business school, Öhringen
Austraße 21
Client: Hohenlohekreis
Architects: Behnisch & Partners
Project architect: Dagmar Schork
Project team: Sandra Seibold, Jürgen Mattmann,
                   Martina Höh

Site supervision:	Sigrid Duffner, Armin Gebert, Wolfgang Leukel
Landscape with:	Hans Luz + Partner

St Benno grammar school, Dresden
Pillnitzer Straße 39

Client:	Bistum Dresden-Meißen
Architects:	Behnisch & Behnisch
	Günter Behnisch, Stefan Behnisch
Project architect:	Martin Werminghausen
Project team:	Felix Bembé, Martina Höh, Jürgen Mattmann, Michael Schuch, Iris Stamminger, Barbara Stölzle
Site Supervision:	Kerstin Bode, Thomas Hoppe, Eva Höhle
Colours:	Erich Wiesner, Berlin
Landscape with:	Büro Noack, Dresden
Lighting engineer:	Walter Bamberger, Pfünz

Sports-hall Am Deutenberg, Schwenningen
Spittelstraße 85

Client:	Stadt Schwenningen
Architects:	Günter Behnisch with Manfred Bacher

Sports-hall of the Oskar von Miller secondary school, Rothenburg ob der Tauber

Client:	Stadt Rothenburg ob der Tauber
Architects:	Behnisch & Partners
Project team:	Lothar Fahrig, Hannes Hübner

Facilities and landscape for the 1972 Olympic Games, Munich
Olympiapark, Spiridon-Louis-Ring

Client:	Bundesrepublik Deutschland, Freistaat Bayern, Stadt München
Overall design:	Behnisch & Partners, Günter Behnisch, Fritz Auer, Winfried Büxel, Erhard Tränkner, Carlo Weber with Jürgen Joedicke
Landscape with:	Günther Grzimek
Roofing:	Behnisch & Partners, Frei Otto, Leonhardt + Andrä
Engineer in charge:	Jörg Schlaich
Visual communication:	Otl Aicher
Design of the main sports facilities:	Behnisch & Partners
Overall project cooperation:	Christian Kandzia, Frohmut Kurz, Hermann Peltz
Exterior areas:	Karla Kowalski, Jürgen Krug, Wendelin Rauch, Udo Welter
Stadium:	Hans Beier (project leader), Horst Friedrichs (project leader), Konrad Müller (project leader), Adolf Schindhelm (project leader), Helmut Beutel, Eberhard Heilmann, Horst Stockburger.
Sports-hall:	Berthold Rosewich (project leader), Gerd Eicher, Wolfgang Illgen, Lothar Hitzig, Jürgen Langer, Lucio Parolini, Ulrich Zahn.
Swimming pools:	Jörg Bauer (project leader), Godfrid Haberer, Peter Rogge, Wilfried Wolf
Roofing:	Johann Albrecht, Horst Stockburger, Cord Wehrse

Training and warm-up hall for Munich Olympics

Client:	Bundesrepublik Deutschland, Freistaat Bayern, Stadt München
Architects:	Behnisch & Partners
Project team:	Godfried Haberer, Horst Stockburger, Hermann Peltz

Auf dem Schäfersfeld sports-hall, Lorch

Client:	Stadt Lorch
Architects:	Behnisch & Partners
Project team:	Hannes Hübner, Peter Kaltschmidt, Hermann Peltz
Site supervision:	Lothar Frey, Lorch

"Glaspalast" sports-hall, Sindelfingen
Rudolf-Harbig-Straße 10

Client:	Stadt Sindelfingen
Architects:	Behnisch & Partners
Projekt architect:	Winfried Büxel (partner)
Co-worker:	Ulrich Kohlleppel
Site supervision:	Sindelfingen Department of Civil Engineering

School sports-hall, Sulzbach an der Murr
Jahnstraße 13

Client:	Gemeinde Sulzbach an der Murr
Architects:	Behnisch & Partners
Project architect:	Wolfgang Vögele

Old people's home and nursing home, Reutlingen
Ringelbachstraße 57–59

Client:	Stadt Reutlingen
Architects:	Behnisch & Partners
Project architect:	Dieter Herrmann
Co-worker:	Klaus-Dieter Keck
Site architect:	Rudolf Lettner

Kindergarten, Stuttgart-Neugereut
Pelikanstraße 26

Client:	Evangelische Kirchengemeinde Stuttgart-Neugereut
Architects:	Behnisch & Partners
Project architect:	Christian Kandzia

Site supervision: Martin Hühn
Kindergarten, Stuttgart-Luginsland
Lotharstraße 24
Client: Landeshauptstadt Stuttgart
Architects: Behnisch & Partners
Project architect: Sibylle Käppel-Klieber
Exterior areas: Landeshauptstadt Stuttgart, Department of Parks and Gardens, Stuttgart
Social housing, Ingolstadt-Hollerstauden
Albertus-Magnus-Straße 9-11
Client: Sankt-Gundekar-Werk Eichstätt, Schwabach
Architects: Günter Behnisch and Manfred Sabatke
Project architect: Christoph Lueder
Project group: Volker Spänle, Rebecca Streckert
Site supervision: Bärbel Riedmüller, Philip Buel
Exterior
areas with: Hans Luz + Partner
Health and spa facilities, Bad Elster
Badstraße 5–7
Client: Sächsische Staatsbäder GmbH, Bad Elster, vertreten durch Staatliches Vermögens- und Hochbauamt, Zwickau
Architects: Günter Behnisch and Manfred Sabatke
Project architect: Christof Jantzen
Project team: Richard Beßler, Nicole Stümper, Michael Blank, Dieter Rehm
Site supervision: CBP Cronauer Beratung and Planung, München
Landscape with: Hans Luz + Partner
Colours: Erich Wiesner, Berlin
Sports and leisure pools, Leipzig-Grünau
Stuttgarter Allee 7
Client: Sport- und Bäderamt Leipzig vertreten durch Hochbauamt Leipzig
Architects: Behnisch, Behnisch & Partner Günter Behnisch, Stefan Behnisch, Günther Schaller
Project architects: Andrea Crumbach, Christine Stroh-Mocek
Project group: Martin Gremmel, Michael Schuch, Eva Höhle
With: Christian Kandzia
Site supervision
with: Erfurth + Partner, Leipzig, Eva Höhle
National Library, Frankfurt am Main
Eckenheimer Landstraße/Adickesallee
Competition design

Client: Bundesrepublik Deutschland
Architects: Behnisch & Partners
Co-workers: Cornelia Theilig, Wolfgang Vögele, Friedhelm Weist, Christian Kandzia, Ulrich Hamann
Hysolar research and institute building of the University of Stuttgart, Stuttgart-Vaihingen
Allmandring 19
Client: Saudi Arabian National Centre for Science and Technology, Bundesministerium für Forschung und Technologie, Ministerium für Wissenschaft und Kunst des Landes Baden-Württemberg, vertreten durch Universitätsbauamt Stuttgart und Hohenheim
Architects: Behnisch & Partners
Project team: Frank Stepper, Arnold Ehrhardt
Library of the Catholic University, Eichstätt
Universitätsallee 1
Client: Stiftung der Katholischen Universität Eichstätt, vertreten durch Universitäts-/Diözesanbauamt
Architects: Behnisch & Partners
Project architects: Manfred Sabatke (partner), Christian Kandzia, Joachim Zürn
Co-workers: Helmut Dasch, Jutta Schürmann, Cornelia Theilig, Birgit Weigel, Thomas Zimmermann
Competition
design: Sabine Behnisch-Staib
Site supervison: Martin Hühn
Landscape with: Hans Luz + Partner
Lighting engineer: Walter Bamberger, Pfünz
Post and Communications Museum, Frankfurt am Main
Schaumainkai 53
Client: Bundesministerium für Post und Fernmeldewesen, vertreten durch Oberpostdirektion Frankfurt
Architects: Behnisch & Partners
Project team: Peter Schürmann (in charge), Felix Heßmert (project architect), Gotthard Geiselmann
Christian Kandzia helped to coordinate the project from summer 1988 to its completion.
Co-workers: Martina Deiss-Eilers, Jochen Hauff, Margit Schosser-Ellensohn
Site supervision: Rudolf Lettner, Martin Hühn, Uwe Sachs, Sigrid Schäfer
Landscape with: Hans Luz + Partner

Akademie der Künste Berlin-Brandenburg, Berlin
Pariser Platz 4
Client: Land Berlin für die Akademie der Künste
Architects: Behnisch & Partner with Werner Durth
Project architects: Franz Harder (project partner), Jochen Schmidt, Matias Stumpfl
Project team: Andreas Ludwig, Bertold Jungblut
Competition design: Ruth Berktold

The Harbourside Centre for the Performing Arts, Bristol, UK
Client: The Harbourside Centre, Bristol/UK
Architects: Behnisch, Behnisch & Partner Günter Behnisch, Stefan Behnisch, Günther Schaller
Project partner: David Cook
Project group: Martin Arvidsson, Volker Biermann, Andreas Ditschuneit, Martin Gremmel, Jill Hauck-Spaeh, Malte Hofmeister, Diana Michael, Frank Ockert, Klaus Schwägerl, Ian Waters

Lothar-Günther Buchheim Museum, Bernried am Starnberger See
Client: Freistaat Bayern, Bayerisches Staatsministerium für Wissenschaft, Forschung und Kunst
Architects: Behnisch, Behnisch & Partner Günter Behnisch, Stefan Behnisch, Günther Schaller
Project architects: Martin Werminghausen (project partner), Roland Stölzle
Co-worker: Roland Zimmermann
Landscape with: Hans Luz + Partner
Lighting engineers: Atelier Bartenbach, Innsbruck

National and Provincial Archives, Copenhagen, Denmark
Ørestad Nord
Client: Ministry of Education Building Directorate, Copenhagen/Denmark
User: Statens Arkiver, Rigsarkivet Copenhagen/Denmark
Architects/Project management: Behnisch, Behnisch & Partner Günter Behnisch, Stefan Behnisch, Günther Schaller
Project management: Ton Gilissen, David Cook (Project leader)
Project architects: Martin Arvidsson, Ton Gilissen, Armin Kammer, Diana Michael, Karin Scholl
Competition design: David Cook, Martin Haas, Trine Berthold
Landscape with: WES Hamburg (competition)

Regional headquarters of the Diakonisches Werk, Stuttgart
Heilbronner Straße 180
Client: Diakonisches Werk der evangelischen Kirche in Württemberg
Architects: Behnisch & Partners
Project architect: Gerald Staib
Co-workers: Astrid Chwoika, Helmut Dasch, Ulrich Hamann
Site architect: Rudolf Lettner
Landscape with: Hans Luz + Partner

Research factory of the Leybold AG, Alzenau
Siemensstraße 100
Client: Leybold AG, Hanau
Architects: Behnisch & Partners
Project group: Andreas Theilig (project partner), Herbert Jötten, Uwe Schindler, Ulrich Liebert
Co-workers: Hubert Eilers, Wolfgang Hinkfoth, Anke Pfudel, Ute Rudolph-Kumpf, Margit Schosser, Ernst-Ulrich Tillmanns
Construction supervision: Ulrich Liebert, Heinz Schröder
Landscape with: Gesswein-Roth-Henkel

Central administration building of the State Clearing Bank of Baden-Württemberg at the Hoppenlau Cemetery, Stuttgart. Competition Design
Client: Landesgirokasse, Stuttgart
Architects: Behnisch & Partners, City Office
Competition and project architects: Stefan Behnisch, Eberhard Pritzer
Project group: Ulrich Mangold, Lür Meyer, Ken Radtkey

Service centre State Clearing Bank of Baden-Württemberg am Bollwerk, Stuttgart
Fritz-Elsas-Straße 31
Client: Landesgirokasse, Grundstücks-

	anlagengesellschaft mbH + Co. KG, Stuttgart
Architects:	Behnisch, Sabatke, Behnisch
Project partner and project architect:	Günther Schaller
Project architects:	Andrea Crumbach, Martin Schodder, Wolfgang Sterr, Thomas Strittmatter
Project group:	Vince Bandy, Volker Biermann, Michael Blank, Julianna Fecskes, Stefanie Flaubert, Ulrich Hanselmann, Rochus Hinkel, Hans-Peter Höhn, Tom Hurt, Peter Koller, Ingrid Marx, Christoph Mayr, Christoph Mischke, Claudia Möller, Laura Rovelli, Birgit Sauerhammer, Bettina Stark, Roland Stölzle, Peter Voelki, Edelgard Wilburger
With:	Christian Kandzia
Facade consultants:	Erich Mosbacher, Friedrichshafen
Landscape with:	Hans Luz + Partner
Lighting engineer:	Walter Bamberger, Pfünz
Site supervision:	Hans-Joachim Maile, Stuttgart

Headquarters of State Insurance in Schleswig-Holstein, Lübeck
Ziegelstraße 150

Client:	Landesversicherungsanstalt Schleswig-Holstein
Architects:	Behnisch & Behnisch
Project architect and project leader:	Gunnar Ramsfjell
Project architects:	Martin Arvidsson, Birger Bhandary, David Cook, Jörn Genkel, Martin Gremmel, Horst Müller, Martina Schaab, Jörg Usinger
Project group:	Elke Altenburger, Thomas Balke, Marc Benz, Iris Bulla, Kathrin Dennig, Jutta Fritsch, Stefan Forrer, Pietro Granaiola, Heiko Krampe, Cecilia Perez, Matthias Schmidt, Timo Saller, Jan Soltau, Georg Taxhet, Karin Weigang
With:	Christian Kandzia
Project management:	Assmann Beraten + Planen, Hamburg
Site supervision:	Behnisch & Behnisch, Cronauer Beratung + Planung, Munich. Bernd Giesen (CBP), Axel Bruchmann, Heiko Krampe, Ulrich Jedelhauser
Landscape:	WES & Partner, Hamburg

Offices and exhibition space for VS, Tauberbischofsheim
Hochhäuser Straße 8

Client:	VS – Vereinigte Spezialmöbelfabriken
Architects:	Behnisch, Behnisch & Partner Günter Behnisch, Stefan Behnisch, Günther Schaller
Project architects:	Volker Biermann, Wolfgang Sterr
Project group:	Martin Arvidsson, Andreas Braun, Dieter Ludwig, Karin Scholl
With:	Christian Kandzia
Site supervision:	Gey + Partner, Tauberbischofsheim
Landscape with:	Hans Luz + Partner, Stuttgart

Pedestrian zone and underground station Königstraße and Schloßplatz, Stuttgart

Client:	Stadt Stuttgart, Land Baden-Württemberg
Architects:	Behnisch & Partners Manfred Sabatke (Project partner), Carlo Weber (Project partner)
Co-workers:	Dr. Ing. Hartmut Niederwöhrmeier, Claudia Häfele, Ingo Ewerth, Heidi Kief
With:	Hans Luz + Partner and City of Stuttgart, Civil Engineering Department

Schloßplatz Underground station, Stuttgart

Client:	Stadt Stuttgart,
Architects:	Behnisch & Partners. Manfred Sabatke (Project partner), Carlo Weber (Project partner)
Co-worker:	Cornelia Henne
With:	City of Stuttgart, Civil Engineering Department

Wiener Platz, Stuttgart-Feuerbach

Client:	Stadt Stuttgart, Tiefbauamt, Abteilung Stadtbahn
Architects:	Behnisch & Partners
Project architects:	Matthias Tusker, Ulrich Mangold

Airport control tower, Nürnberg
Flughafenstraße 100

Client:	Flughafen Nürnberg GmbH
Architects:	Günter Behnisch and Manfred Sabatke
Projects architects:	Armin Kammer (project leader), Alexander Schleifenheimer, Markus Hilpert

Co-workers:	Julia Boedeker, Norbert Erb, Tobias Hegemann, Gabriele von Lorenz, Susanne Pfeiffer, Britta Kohler, Alexander Rottmaier, Anne-Claire von Braunmühl
Site supervision:	Henrik Vogt, Tanja Schmidt
Competition team:	Petra Venzke, Joachim Daller
Landscape with:	Werkgemeinschaft Freiraum, Nürnberg

New federal buildings and their integration in the city of Bonn

Competition design:	1973
design development:	1974 and 1975
Client:	Deutscher Bundestag
Architects:	Behnisch & Partners
Project group:	Fritz Auer (partner), Carlo Weber (partner), Christian Kandzia, Fromuth Kurz, Horst Stockburger, Dieter Herrmann
Landscape with:	Günther Grzimek

Federal Buildings Bonn. Urban considerations with "Green Centre".

Design:	1979
Architects:	Behnisch & Partners
Project partner:	Fritz Auer
Landscape with:	Günther Grzimek

Plenary Complex of the German Bundestag, Bonn
Görresstraße

Client:	Deutscher Bundestag, represented by Bundesbaudirektion Bonn
Architects:	Behnisch & Partners
Project partner and project architect:	Gerald Staib
Project architects:	Hubert Eilers, Matthias Burkart, Eberhard Pritzer, Alexander von Salmuth, Ernst-Ulrich Tillmanns
In co-operation with:	Christian Kandzia
Project team:	Steffi Georg, Bernd Linder, Falk Petry, Jürgen Steffens, Alexander von Padberg
Co-workers:	Till-Markus Bauer, Simon Eisinger, Ralf Helmer, Armin Kammer, Susan Kayser, Götz Klieber, Dieter Kowalczik, Achim Kulla, Ansgar Lamott, Bettina Maier, Eckard Mauch, Carmen Müller, Martina Nadansky, Anke Pfudel, Rolf Scheddel-Mohr, Kay von Scholley, Martin Volz, Matthias Wichmann, Carola Wiese, Jens Wittfoth
Site supervision:	Ulrich Liebert, Heinz Schröder, Bernd Troske
Co-workers:	Gabriele Hartmann, Peter Kling, Kai Kniesel, Karl-Heinz Soboll
Landscape with:	Hans Luz + Partner

Werkverzeichnis / List of buildings and projects

Bauten und Projekte, die in diesem Buch vorgestellt werden, sind in dieser Zusammenstellung durch Fettdruck hervorgehoben.

Buildings and projects presented in this book are set in bold type.

1954	Kreishandelsschule, jetzt Schiller-Realschule* Schwäbisch Gmünd		1954	District business school, today Schiller secondary school* Schwäbisch Gmünd
1956	Hans-Baldung-Gymnasium* Schwäbisch Gmünd		1956	Hans Baldung grammar school* Schwäbisch Gmünd
1957	Landratsamt* Schwäbisch Gmünd		1957	District President's Office* Schwäbisch Gmünd
1958	Heilig-Kreuz-Kirche* Stuttgart-Sommerrain. Zerstört		1958	Holy Cross Church* Stuttgart-Sommerrain. Demolished
1958	Grund- und Hauptschule* Stuttgart-Sommerrain		1958	Primary and secondary school* Stuttgart-Sommerrain
1958	Berufsschule** Radolfzell		1958	Vocational school** Radolfzell
1959	**Hohenstaufen-Gymnasium* Göppingen**		**1959**	**Hohenstaufen grammar school * Göppingen**
1960	Berufsschule** Radolfzell		1960	Vocational school ** Radolfzell
1960	Volksschule* Lorch/Württemberg		1960	Primary school* Lorch/Württemberg
1961	**Vogelsangschule* Stuttgart**		**1961**	**Vogelsang school* Stuttgart**
1963	**Staatliche Fachhochschule für Technik* Ulm an der Donau**		**1963**	**Ulm engineering school* Ulm on Donau**
1964	Golden-Bühl-Schule** Villingen		1964	Golden Bühl school** Villingen
1964	Montageschule Heidenheim		1964	Prefabricated system school Heidenheim
1965	Montageschule** Radolfzell		1965	Prefabricated system school** Radolfzell
1965	Montageschule** Villingen		1965	Prefabricated system school** Villingen
1965	**Progymnasium, jetzt Hauptschule** Furtwangen**		**1965**	**Grammar school, today secondary modern school** Furtwangen**
1965	Gymnasium am Deutenberg** Schwenningen		1965	Deutenberg grammar school** Schwenningen
1965	Grundschule Alfdorf		1965	Primary school Alfdorf
1965	Hauptschule Dettingen/Teck		1965	Secondary school Dettingen/Teck
1965	Volksschule*** Geislingen		1965	Primary school*** Geislingen

1965	Schulzentrum*** Haigerloch		1965	School complex*** Haigerloch
1966	Droste-Hülshoff-Gymnasium Freiburg		1966	Droste Hülshoff grammar school Freiburg
1966	Volksschule*** Engstlatt		1966	Primary school*** Engstlatt
1966	Friedrich-von-Keller-Schule*** Ludwigsburg-Neckarweihingen		1966	Friedrich von Keller school*** Ludwigsburg-Neckarweihingen
1966	Erweiterung Volksschule und Turnhalle** Steißlingen		1966	Extension of primary school and sports-hall** Steißlingen
1967	Ferienhaus Fink Schlechtbach		1967	Fink vacation house Schlechtbach
1968	Staatliche Fachhochschule Aalen		1968	State technical college Aalen
1968	Saliergymnasium Waiblingen		1968	Salier grammar school Waiblingen
1969	Wohnhaus Behnisch Ostfildern-Kemnat		1969	Behnisch house Ostfildern-Kemnat
1969	Pavillon im Gelände der Bundesgartenschau Dortmund		1969	Pavilion in the Federal Garden Exhibition Dortmund
1969	Verwaltungsgebäude der Zentralkasse der Viehbesitzer Stuttgart		1969	Administration building of the Central Bank of Cattle Owners Stuttgart
1969	Anne-Frank-Schule** Furtwangen		1969	Anne Frank school** Furtwangen
1969	**Mittelpunktschule und Sporthalle «In den Berglen» bei Oppelsbohm**		**1969**	**School and sports-hall "In den Berglen" near Oppelsbohm**
1969	Oskar-von-Miller-Realschule Rothenburg ob der Tauber		1969	Oskar von Miller secondary school Rothenburg ob der Tauber
1969	Theodor-Heuss-Gymnasium und Turnhalle** Schopfheim		1969	Theodor Heuss grammar school and sports-hall** Schopfheim
1969	Wohnhaus Gackstatter und Seth Stuttgart-Weilimdorf		1969	Gackstatter and Seth house Stuttgart-Weilimdorf
1969	**Sporthalle Schwenningen**		**1969**	**Sports-hall Schwenningen**
1970	Friedrich-Schiller-Gymnasium Marbach am Neckar		1970	Friedrich Schiller grammar school Marbach am Neckar
1970	Realschule West Ludwigsburg		1970	Secondary School West Ludwigsburg
1970	Saliersporthalle «Auf der Korber Höhe» Waiblingen		1970	Salier sports-hall "Auf der Korber Höhe" Waiblingen
1970	**Sporthalle bei der Oskar-von-Miller-Realschule Rothenburg ob der Tauber**		**1970**	**Sports-hall near Oskar von Miller secondary school Rothenburg ob der Tauber**
1970	Bürogebäude Mendelssohnstraße 22 Stuttgart-Sillenbuch. Zerstört.		1970	Office building Mendelssohnstraße 22 Stuttgart-Sillenbuch. Demolished
1970	Wohngebäude Treitschkestraße Stuttgart-Sillenbuch		1970	Apartment building Treitschkestraße Stuttgart-Sillenbuch
1970	Heim der Hymnus-Chorknaben Stuttgart		1970	Home of the Hymnus Choir Boys Stuttgart

1972	Ergänzungsgebäude Saliergymnasium und Neubau Realschule Schulzentrum «Rechts der Rems» Waiblingen	1972	Extension Salier grammar school and new construction of secondary school School complex "Rechts der Rems" Waiblingen
1972	Ladenzentrum und Bibliothek Ulm-Böfingen	1972	Shops and library Ulm-Böfingen
1972	**Bauten und Anlagen für die Spiele der XX. Olympiade Olympiapark mit Stadion, Sporthalle, Schwimmhalle, Aufwärmhalle und temporären Bauten für die Besucherversorgung München**	**1972**	**Buildings and facilities for the XX. Olympic Games. Olympiapark with stadium, sports-hall, swimming pools, warm-up hall and temporary buildings for visitor services Munich**
1972	Gymnasium und Sporthalle** Radolfzell	1972	Grammar school and sports-hall** Radolfzell
1973	**Progymnasium und Realschule «Auf dem Schäfersfeld» Lorch/Württemberg**	**1973**	**"Auf dem Schäfersfeld" grammar school and secondary school Lorch/Württemberg**
1974	Josef-Effner-Gymnasium Dachau	1974	Josef Effner grammar school Dachau
1975	Hauptschule und Sporthalle «Bei der Bleiche» Rothenburg ob der Tauber	1975	"Bei der Bleiche" secondary school and sports-hall Rothenburg ob der Tauber
1976	**Sporthalle «Auf dem Schäfersfeld» Lorch/Württemberg**	**1976**	**"Auf dem Schäfersfeld" sports-hall Lorch/Württemberg**
1976	Bildungszentrum am Salinensee** Bad Dürrheim	1976	Salinensee educational complex** Bad Dürrheim
1976	**Fritz-Erler-Schule Pforzheim**	**1976**	**Fritz Erler school Pforzheim**
1976	Verwaltungsgebäude für die Münchner Olympiapark GmbH München	1976	Administration building for Münchner Olympiapark GmbH Munich
1977	**Sporthalle «Glaspalast» Sindelfingen**	**1977**	**"Glaspalast" sports-hall Sindelfingen**
1977	**Kindergarten Pelikanstraße Stuttgart-Neugereut**	**1977**	**Kindergarten Pelikanstraße Stuttgart-Neugereut**
1977	**Alten- und Pflegeheim Ringelbachstraße Reutlingen**	**1977**	**Old people's home and nursing home Ringelbachstraße Reutlingen**
1978	**U-Bahn-Station «Schloßplatz» Stuttgart**	**1978**	**"Schloßplatz" underground station Stuttgart**
1978	Reichsstadt-Gymnasium Rothenburg ob der Tauber	1978	Reichsstadt grammar school Rothenburg ob der Tauber
1979	Sporthalle Ludwigsburg-Neckarweihingen	1979	Sports-hall Ludwigsburg-Neckarweihingen
1979	**Studien- und Ausbildungszentrum der Evangelischen Landeskirche in Württemberg Stuttgart-Birkach**	**1979**	**Schooling and training centre of the Württemberg Protestant Church Stuttgart-Birkach**
1980	**Fußgängerbereich Untere und Obere Königstraße, Marienstraße und Kleine Königstraße. Neugestaltung Schloßplatz,**	**1980**	**Pedestrian zone Untere und Obere Königstraße, Marienstraße and Kleine Königstraße. New design Schloßplatz,**

	Planie und Karlsplatz Stuttgart		Planie and Karlsplatz Stuttgart
1980	Erweiterung der Grund- und Hauptschule Alfdorf	1980	Extension of primary and secondary school Alfdorf
1981	Gewerbliches Bildungszentrum Balthasar-Neumann-Schulen Bruchsal	1981	Centre for trade schools Balthasar Neumann Schools Bruchsal
1981	Erweiterung Friedrich-Schiller-Gymnasium Marbach am Neckar	1981	Extension of Friedrich Schiller grammar school Marbach am Neckar
1982	**Hauptschule «Auf dem Schäfersfeld» Lorch/Württemberg**	**1982**	**"Auf dem Schäfersfeld" secondary school, Lorch/Württemberg**
1982	Sporthalle Reutlingen-Storlach	1982	Sports-hall Reutlingen-Storlach
1982	Altenpflegeheim «August-Kayser-Stiftung» Pforzheim	1982	"August-Kayser-Stiftung" nursing home Pforzheim
1983	Haus- und landwirtschaftliche Berufsschule Herrenberg	1983	Domestic science and agricultural trade School Herrenberg
1984	**Landesgeschäftsstelle der Ev. Landeskirche des Diakonischen Werkes in Württemberg Stuttgart**	**1984**	**Regional headquarters of the Protestant Church of the Diakonisches Werk (religions charity) in Württemberg Stuttgart**
1984	**Sporthalle Sulzbach an der Murr**	**1984**	**Sports-hall Sulzbach on Murr**
1985	Erweiterung Fachhochschule für Technik Ulm an der Donau	1985	Extension of Ulm engineering school Ulm on Donau
1986	Aufstockung eines Analysengebäudes der Leybold AG Hanau	1986	Vertical addition to a laboratory building of the Leybold AG Hanau
1986	Sporthalle für die Balthasar-Neumann-Schulen Bruchsal	1986	Sports-hall for Balthasar Neumann schools Bruchsal
1987	**Zentralbibliothek der Katholischen Universität Eichstätt**	**1987**	**Main library for the Catholic University Eichstätt**
1987	**Hysolar Forschungs- und Institutsgebäude der Universität Stuttgart Stuttgart-Vaihingen**	**1987**	**Hysolar research and institute building of the University of Stuttgart Stuttgart-Vaihingen**
1987	Büro-, Labor- und Produktionsgebäude der Leybold AG, Hanau Alzenau	1987	Office, laboratory and production building for Leybold AG, Hanau Alzenau
1990	Museum für Post und Kommunikation Frankfurt am Main	1990	Post and Communications Museum Frankfurt on Main
1990	Kindergarten Lotharstraße Stuttgart-Luginsland	1990	Kindergarten Lotharstraße Stuttgart-Luginsland
1991	Neugestaltung des Bahnhofsvorplatzes Stuttgart-Feuerbach	1991	New design of station square Stuttgart-Feuerbach
1991	Albert-Schweitzer-Schule Bad Rappenau	1991	Albert Schweitzer school Bad Rappenau

1991	Erweiterung der Stauferschule Lorch/Württemberg		1991	Extension of Staufer school Lorch/Württemberg
1991	Erweiterungsgebäude für die Gießerei, Roboter- und Sensortechnik der Fachhochschule Aalen		1991	Extension of foundry, robotics- and sensor technology of Technical College Aalen
1992	**Plenar- und Präsidialbereich des Deutschen Bundestages Bonn**		**1992**	**Plenary and presidential areas of the German Parliament Bonn**
1993	Wohnhaus Charlotte am Silberwald Stuttgart-Sillenbuch		1993	Charlotte Silberwald house Stuttgart-Sillenbuch
1993	Umbau und Sanierung des Gemeindehauses Atrium Gorch-Fock-Straße 30 Stuttgart-Sillenbuch		1993	Alteration and renovation of Municipal Building Atrium Gorch-Fock-Straße 30 Stuttgart-Sillenbuch
1993	**Kaufmännische Schule und Sporthalle Öhringen**		**1993**	**Business school and sports-hall Öhringen**
1994	**Erweiterung des Progymnasiums und der Realschule Lorch/Württemberg**		**1994**	**Extension to grammar school and secondary school Lorch/Württemberg**
1994	Ergänzungsgebäude der Landesgeschäftsstelle des Diakonischen Werkes Stuttgart		1994	Addition to State Offices of the Diakonisches Werk Stuttgart
1994	Geschwister-Scholl-Schule Frankfurt am Main		1994	Geschwister Scholl school Frankfurt on Main
1996	Münsterkindergarten Ingolstadt-Hollerstauden		1996	Kindergarten of Münster parish Ingolstadt-Hollerstauden
1996	Umbau des Bürogebäudes Kronprinzstraße 22 der Bayerischen Vereinsbank Stuttgart		1996	Alteration of office building Kronprinzstraße 22 of Bayerische Vereinsbank Stuttgart
1996	**St. Benno-Gymnasium Dresden** Behnisch & Behnisch		**1996**	**St Benno grammar school Dresden** Behnisch & Behnisch
1996	Werkstätten für die Olympiapark München GmbH München		1996	Workshops for Olympiapark München GmbH Munich
1996	Montessorischule Ingolstadt-Hollerstauden		1996	Montessori school Ingolstadt-Hollerstauden
1996	**Theater- und Konzerthalle Bristol / UK** Behnisch, Behnisch & Partner		**1996**	**Arts centre Bristol / UK** Behnisch, Behnisch & Partner
1997	**Dienstleistungsgebäude am Bollwerk für die Landesgirokasse Stuttgart** Behnisch, Sabatke, Behnisch		**1997**	**Bollwerk service building for the Landesgirokasse Stuttgart** Behnisch, Sabatke, Behnisch
1997	**Landesversicherungsanstalt Schleswig-Holstein Lübeck** Behnisch & Behnisch		**1997**	**State Insurance of Schleswig Holstein Lübeck** Behnisch & Behnisch
1997	**Wohnanlage Albertus-Magnus-Straße Ingolstadt-Hollerstauden**		**1997**	**Residential complex Albertus-Magnus-Straße Ingolstadt-Hollerstauden**

1998	Aufbereitungsgebäude für Kaltmoor Bad Elster		1998	Treatment building, health spa Bad Elster
1998	IBN-Institutsgebäude für Forst- und Naturforschung Wageningen/NL Behnisch & Behnisch		1998	IBN-Institute Building for Research in Forestry and Nature Wageningen/NL Behnisch & Behnisch
1998	**Büro- und Ausstellungsgebäude der Firma VS Tauberbischofsheim** Behnisch, Behnisch & Partner		**1998**	**Office and exhibition building for VS Company Tauberbischofsheim** Behnisch, Behnisch & Partner
1998	**Kontrollturm für den Flughafen Nürnberg**		**1998**	**Control tower for Nuremberg airport**
1998	Haus Wegmann Ingolstadt-Gerolfing		1998	Wegmann house Ingolstadt-Gerolfing
1998	Sporthalle für die Montessorischule Ingolstadt-Hollerstauden		1998	Montessori school Sports-hall Ingolstadt-Hollerstauden
1999	**Sport- und Freizeitbad «Grünauer Welle» Leipzig-Grünau** Behnisch, Behnisch & Partner		**1999**	**Sports and leisure pools "Grünauer Welle" Leipzig-Grünau** Behnisch, Behnisch & Partner
1999	**Erweiterung und Umbau des Kurmittelhauses Bad Elster**		**1999**	**Extension and alteration of spa buildings Bad Elster**
2000	**Lothar-Günther-Buchheim-Museum Bernried am Starnberger See** Behnisch, Behnisch & Partner		**2000**	**Lothar-Günther Buchheim Museum Bernried on Starnberger See** Behnisch, Behnisch & Partner
2001	Technologiegebäude der Technischen Universität Ilmenau Behnisch, Behnisch & Partner		2001	Technology building of the Technical University Ilmenau Behnisch, Behnisch & Partner
2001	Theodor-Heuss-Haus Stuttgart		2001	Theodor Heuss building Stuttgart
2001	Wohn- und Geschäftshaus Peters- und Lohstraße Krefeld		2001	Residential and office building Peters and Lohstraße Krefeld
2001	Restaurant in der Olympia-Schwimmhalle München		2001	Restaurant in the Olympic Swimming Hall Munich
2001	Europäisches Berufsbildungswerk mit Schulungsgebäude, Wohn- und Sportanlagen Bitburg		2001	European Vocational Training Centre with classroom building, dormitory and sports facilities Bitburg
2002	Norddeutsche Landesbank am Friedrichswall Hannover Behnisch, Behnisch & Partner		2002	Norddeutsche Landesbank Friedrichswall Hanover Behnisch, Behnisch & Partner
2002	«nova home», Firmensitz der nova data AG Ettlingen Behnisch, Behnisch & Partner		2002	"nova home", headquarters of nova data AG Ettlingen Behnisch, Behnisch & Partner
2002	Erweiterung des Hotels Adlon an der Behrenstraße Berlin Behnisch & Partner mit Werner Durth		2002	Extension of Hotel Adlon on Behrenstraße Berlin Behnisch & Partner with Werner Durth

2002	**Akademie der Künste** **Berlin-Brandenburg** **Berlin** Behnisch & Partner mit Werner Durth		2002	**Akademie der Künste** **Berlin-Brandenburg** **Berlin** Behnisch & Partner with Werner Durth
2004	**Dänisches Staatsarchiv** **Kopenhagen/DN** Behnisch, Behnisch & Partner		2004	**Danish State Archives** **Copenhagen/DN** Behnisch, Behnisch & Partner

In Zusammenarbeit mit
* Bruno Lambart, ** Lothar Seidel, *** Horst Bidlingmeier

In cooperation with
* Bruno Lambart, ** Lothar Seidel, *** Horst Bidlingmeier

Ausgewählte Bibliographie / Selective bibliography

Carl Heinz Harbeke und Christian Kandzia, «Bauten für Olympia '72». Harbeke Verlag, München, 1972.

«The Munich Tensile Structures». Zodiak 21, Milano, September 1972.

«Behnisch & Partner. Bauten und Entwürfe 1952–1974». Ed.: Christian Kandzia. Verlag Gerd Hatje, Stuttgart, 1975 and 1983.

Toshia Nakamura, «Behnisch and Partners». Architecture + Urbanism, Tokyo, September 1973.

Heinrich Klotz, «Architektur in der Bundesrepublik. Gespräche mit Günter Behnisch u. a.». Verlag Ullstein, Frankfurt/Main, Berlin, Wien, 1977.

Günter Behnisch, «Offenheit und Vielfalt». Special issue on Behnisch & Partner. db-deutsche bauzeitung 3/1982, Deutsche Verlagsanstalt, Stuttgart, 1982.

Günter Behnisch, «Das Neue ist nicht das Alte» oder «Schräg ist die Tendenz». db-deutsche bauzeitung, 9/1987, Deutsche Verlagsanstalt, Stuttgart, 1987.

Toshio Nakamura, «Special Feature: Günter Behnisch». Architecture + Urbanism 236, Tokyo, May 1990.

Yukio Futagawa, «Postmuseum Frankfurt am Main». GA Document 31 – Global Architecture, 11/1991.

Christian Kandzia, editor, «Behnisch & Partner. Designs 1952–1987». Edition Cantz, Stuttgart, 1991.

Yukio Futagawa, «Special School: Albert Schweitzer-Schule, Bad Rappenau». GA Document 34 – Global Architecture, 9/1992.

«Behnisch & Partner». Bauten 1952–1992». Catalogue of the retrospective at the Galerie der Stadt Stuttgart. Verlag Gerd Hatje, Stuttgart, 1992.

Behnisch & Partner, «Über das Farbliche – On Colour». Verlag Gerd Hatje, Stuttgart, 1993.

Behnisch & Partner, «A Walk through the Exhibition». Verlag Gerd Hatje, Stuttgart, 1994.

Toshio Nakamura, «Günter Behnisch, Behnisch & Partners. Recent Works. Plenary Complex of the German Bundestag». Architecture + Urbanism 291, Tokyo, December 1994.

Yukio Futagawa, «Extension of the Geschwister-Scholl-School, Frankfurt am Main. Vocational School Öhringen». GA Document 42 – Global Architecture, 1/1995.

«Günter Behnisch». Korean Architects, 146, Architecture & Environment Publications, Seoul, Korea, October 1996.

«Behnisch & Partner. Bauten und Projekte 1987–1997». Verlag Gerd Hatje, Ostfildern, 1996.

Alessandra Battisti, Fabrizio Tucci, «Behnisch & Partner. Riflessi di architettura». Parametro 210, 10/1995, Bologna, 1996.

Luigi Biscogli, Alessandra Battisti, Fabrizio Tucci et al, «Günter Behnisch & Partners 1966–1996. 10 opere scelte». Ricerca e Progretto 7/1996, Università degli Studi di Roma «La Sapienza», Roma, 1996.

«Deutscher Bundestag. Acht Fotografen sehen den neuen Plenarbereich des Deutschen Bundestags in Bonn». Edition Braus, Heidelberg, 1996.

Ingrid Mössinger, «Günter Behnisch zum 75. Geburtstag. Eine Festschrift». Städtische Kunstsammlungen, Chemnitz, 1997.

Dominique Gauzin-Müller, «Behnisch & Partners. 50 Years of Architecture». Academy Editions, London, 1997.

Dominique Gauzin-Müller, «Behnisch & Partner. 50 Jahre Architektur». Verlag Ernst & Sohn, Berlin, 1997.

Günter Behnisch, «Der Pariser Platz. Die Akademie der Künste». Jovis-Verlagsbüro, Berlin, 1997.

Luigi Biscogli, «Günter Behnisch – Poetica situazionale». Testo & Immagine, Torino, 1998.

John Reynolds (introduction), «Günter Behnisch – Behnisch & Partners – Behnisch, Behnisch & Partner». Context, Korean Architects, Seoul, Korea (under preparation).

Günter Behnisch, Interview (Klaus-Dieter Weiß), «Verwerfungen des Alltags», Werk, Bauen + Wohnen, Zürich, September 1990.

Klaus-Dieter Weiß, «Freiheit ästhetisieren», DBZ-Deutsche Bauzeitschrift, Gütersloh, Januar 1991.

Arjen Ostermann, «Recent werk van Behnisch & Partner», ARCHIS, Amsterdam, 5/1991.

Editiones ATRIUM S. A., «German Postal Museum. Kindergarten Luginsland», Barcelona, 1991.

Claes Caldenby, «Tyskland Genom 5», arkitektur no. 5, Stockholm, July/August 1993.

Jens Hvass and Morton Jacob Hansen, Interview with Günter Behnisch, ARKITEKTEN 15, Copenhagen, October 1993.

Francisco Asensio Cerver, «Masters: Alzenau factory, Eichstätt university library, Hysolar institute building», Atrium international, Barcelona, 1996.

Lene Dammand Jensen, «Behnisch, Behnisch & Partner Architekten», ARKITEKTEN 05, Copenhagen, March 1997.

AA files 33, «Behnisch & Partner, St. Benno Roman Catholic School, State Insurance Agency Schleswig-Holstein, Central Administration Building, Landesgirokasse», London, Summer 1997.

Fransisco Asensio Cerver, «Deutscher Bundestag», European Masters 11, arco editorial s. a., Barcelona, 1997.

Fabio Quici, «Behnisch, Behnisch & Partner», il PROGETTO, Trieste/Roma, no. 3, 1998.

Dominique Gauzin-Müller, «De la structure porteuse aux structures démultipliées», Techniques et Architecture, Paris, 4/1998.

Egbert Koster, «Natuur onder architectuure», IBN-DLO Wageningen, Schuyt & Co, Haarlem, 1998.

Sarah Wigglesworth and Jeremy Till, «The Everyday and Architecture. Günter Behnisch – Circumstantial Architecture», ARCHITECTURAL DESIGN PROFILE No 134, London, 1998.

«Architekten in Baden-Württemberg», Verlag Buch + Film P. Diemer, Wiesbaden, 1998.

Maritz Vandenberg, «Cable Nets», Olympic Park Roof, Academy Editions, Chichester, 1998.

Gala Abada, «Günter Behnisch. 50 years of innovative, humanistic architecture», medina, issue 9, Heliopolis/Egypt, September/October 1999.

Behnisch, Behnisch & Partner, «Das Bristol Projekt. The Harbourside Centre for Performing Arts», Cantz, Ostfildern, 1999.

Annette LeCuyer, «Radical Tectonics», Thames & Hudson, London, 2000.

Publications of Peter Blundell Jones on Behnisch works

Architects Journal 24/9/86, p 60 – 74. «Modern schools of thought,» criticism and detailed analysis of Hauptschule at Lorch.

Architectural Review (A. R.) March 1988, p 28 – 36. «Behnisch Eichstätt,» criticism of new university library.

A. R. March 1988, p 37 – 41. «Behnisch Hysolar,» criticism of solar institute, University Stuttgart.

A. R. June 88, p 8. «Organic leaders,» review of Behnisch and Partners: designs 1952 – 1987, edited by Christian Kandzia.

A. R. August 88, p 20 – 28. «Alzenau spine,» criticism of factory building near Frankfurt.

Architects Journal 3/5/89, p 76 – 77. «Social structures», review of Behnisch exhibition at Brighton Festival.

A. + U. May 90, 236, p 112 – 121. «Günter Behnisch and Partners: a continuing contribution to the Organic Tradition in German Modernism,» lead essay for special feature on Behnisch work.

A. R. June 90, p 38 – 47. «Post on the Main,» criticism of Post Museum in Frankfurt.

A. R. February 91, p 63 – 72. «Behnisch sports,» retrospective article about sports halls between 1989 and 1996.

A. R. September 91, p 52 – 57. «Kindergarten at Stuttgart-Luginsland.»

A. R. February 92, p 26 – 32. «Good Bad Rappenau,» criticism of a school for children with learning difficulties.

A. R. February 92, p 33 – 36. «Collage place,» criticism of an urban planning project.

«Behnisch und die Architektur des Abenteuers: Eine Betrachtung von jenseits des Kanals.» Catalogue essay in «Behnisch & Partner, Bauten 1952 – 1992,» p 21 – 26, for an exhibition at the Galerie der Stadt Stuttgart, September 1992.

A. R. March 1993, p 20 – 33. «Der Bundestag,» analytical article on the new Parliament.

A. R. April 1995, p 24 – 37. «Behnisch schools,» article on schools at Frankfurt and Öhringen.

Architectural Research Quarterly, winter 1995, p 42 – 49. «The influence of Hans Scharoun,» lecture by Günter Behnisch in connection with the Scharoun Exhibition commissioned and edited by PBJ.

Architects Journal 11, April 1996, p 18/19. «The creative principal,» profile of Günter Behnisch.

Korean Architects 146, 1996, p 37 – 43. «Introduction to the works of Günter Behnisch & Partners.»

A. R. April 1997, p 45 – 49, «Evangelical mission,» article on new offices for the Diakonisches Werk in Stuttgart.

A. R. January 1998, p 60 – 65. «Radical Engagement,» article on Landesgirokasse administration building in Stuttgart.

Glass Technolgy International, May/June 1998, p 170 – 173. «Radical Engagement,» re-run of article on Behnisch Bank (no. 346).

A. R. December 1998, p 41 – 45. «Harbour Master,» article on concert hall project for Bristol by Behnisch, Behnisch & Partners.

Bildnachweis / Illustration Credits

Die Abbildungen stammen aus den Archiven Behnisch & Partner / Behnisch, Behnisch & Partner, Stuttgart; die Fotos des Autors hat dieser zur Verfügung gestellt.

Illustrations are taken from the archives Behnisch & Partners / Behnisch, Behnisch & Partner, Stuttgart; the author provided his own photographs.

Günter Behnisch: 15 bottom
Peter Blundell Jones: 53 (2), 55 bottom, 57 top, 92 top, 96, 112 bottom, 115 bottom, 116, 118 bottom, 147 bottom, 163 bottom, 164 top
Staatsbauamt Frankfurt am Main: 104
Reinhard Friedrich: 16
Ewald Glesmann: 67
Christian Kandzia: front cover, 2, 17, 18,19, 36, 38 (2), 48, 49 (3), 50 (2), 54, 55 top, 56, 57 bottom, 59 (2), 60 (3), 62, 63, 64, 68, 69 top, 71 (2), 72 (3), 73, 74 (2), 75, 77 (3), 78, 79, 80 (2), 81 (2), 82, 83 (2), 85, 86 (4), 87 (2), 89 (3), 91 (2), 92 bottom, 93 (3), 94, 95 (2), 98, 99 (3), 100 (2), 101, 102, 103 (3), 105, 107 (2), 108 (2), 109 (2), 111, 112 top, 113 (3), 114, 115 top, 117 (2), 118 top, 120 (2), 122, 123, 125 (2), 128, 129 (2), 133 (2), 135 (2), 136, 137 (3), 138, 139 (2), 140, 141 (2), 143, 147 top, 148 (2), 151 (2), 152 (2), 153 (2), 154 (2), 156 middle, 157, 158, 159 (3), 160, 163 top, 164 bottom, 165, 166, 167 (2), 169 (2), 172 (2), 173, 175 (2), 176, 177 top, 178 top, 179
Rüdiger Kramm: 15 top, 35, 39 top
Dr. Lassen + Co: 31 bottom
Franz Lazi junior: 10
Lür Meyer: 61
NOP, München-Essen: 70 top
Frank Ockert: 126, 127, 130
OMG, München: 70 bottom
Gottfried Planck: 29 (2), 32 (2), 33, 34
Luftbild Max Prugger: 12, passed by Reg. v. Obb.G30/07187, 69 bottom, passed by Reg. v. Obb.G30/7198
W. Reinhold: 26, 27
Archiv Rostan, Abteilung Montagebau: 11, 31 top
Landeshauptstadt Stuttgart, Ute Schmidt-Contag: 161 (2)
Martin Schodder: 131, 132, 145 (2), 155, 156 top and bottom, 177 bottom, 178 bottom
Wilfried Täubner: 168

Über den Autor / On the author

Peter Blundell Jones studierte Architektur an der Architectural Association in London. Seine berufliche Laufbahn bis heute umfaßt Architekturpraxis, -kritik und -theorie. 1973–74 schrieb er sein erstes Buch über Hans Scharoun und ist seither ein Spezialist auf diesem Gebiet der deutschen Architektur; 1995 erschien sein zweites Buch über Scharoun, 1999 ein weiteres über dessen Kollegen und Mentor Hugo Häring. Blundell Jones' akademische Karriere begann 1978 als Assistent in Cambridge, fand ihre Fortsetzung mit der Lehre an der South Bank University in London und seit 1994 einer Professur für Architektur an der University of Sheffield, wo er die geisteswissenschaftliche Abteilung leitet.

Blundell Jones pflegt eine enge Verbindung mit The Architectural Review und anderen führenden Architekturzeitschriften, unter ihnen Spazio e Società, deren britischer Korrespondent er ist. Er erhielt 1985 den Preis des CICA (Comité international des critiques d'architecture) für den «Besten Zeitschriftenbeitrag der vergangenen drei Jahre» und 1992 die Auszeichnung «Architekturjournalist des Jahres». Zu seinen wichtigsten Themen gehören die englische Arts and Crafts-Bewegung, die schwedischen Architekten Gunnar Asplund und Sigurd Lewerentz sowie die aktuelle Szene in Graz, über die als erstes Buch soeben sein Werk Dialogues in Time: New Graz Architecture (deutsche Ausgabe in Vorbereitung) erschienen ist.

Peter Blundell Jones was trained as an architect at the Architectural Association London. He has been involved throughout his career in practice, criticism and theory. In 1973–74 he wrote his first book on Hans Scharoun, and he has remained an expert on this area of German architecture, producing a second book on Scharoun published in 1995 and another on his colleague and mentor Hugo Häring in 1999. His academic career began with an Assistant Lectureship at Cambridge in 1978 and advanced with a Readership at South Bank University in London. Since 1994 he has been Professor of architecture at the University of Sheffield, where he is in charge of humanities.

Blundell Jones has enjoyed a close working relationship with The Architectural Review and other leading architectural magazines including Spazio e Società, for which he is British correspondent. He received the CICA Award for the "Best periodical of the last three years" in 1985, and was "Architectural Journalist of the Year" in 1992. He has written extensively on the English Arts and Crafts movement, on the Swedish architects Gunnar Asplund and Sigurd Lewerentz, and he recently produced the first book on the recent architectural movement in Graz, Austria, entitled Dialogues in Time: New Graz Architecture.

Große Architekten in der erfolgreichen Studiopaperback-Reihe:
The Work of the World's Great Architects:

Tadao Ando
Masao Furuyama
3., erweiterte Auflage,
248 Seiten,
397 Abbildungen
ISBN 3-7643-5437-2
deutsch / englisch

Atelier 5
216 Seiten,
397 Abbildungen
ISBN 3-7643-6243-X
deutsch / englisch

Gottfried Böhm
Wolfgang Pehnt
176 Seiten,
250 Abbildungen
ISBN 3-7643-5965-X
deutsch / englisch

Mario Botta
Emilio Pizzi
3., erweiterte Auflage,
264 Seiten,
666 Abbildungen
ISBN 3-7643-5438-0
deutsch / französisch

Herman Hertzberger
Herman van Bergeijk
216 Seiten,
330 Abbildungen
ISBN 3-7643-5698-7
deutsch / englisch

Herzog & de Meuron
Wilfried Wang
3., erweiterte Auflage,
216 Seiten,
400 Abbildungen
ISBN 3-7643-5617-0
deutsch / englisch

Philip Johnson
Peter Blake
256 Seiten,
270 Abbildungen
ISBN 3-7643-5393-7
deutsch / englisch

Louis I. Kahn
Klaus-Peter Gast,
192 Seiten,
300 Abbildungen
ISBN 3-7643-5964-1
deutsch / englisch

Richard Meier
Silvio Cassarà
208 Seiten,
264 Abbildungen.
ISBN 3-7643-5350-3

Ludwig Mies van der Rohe
Werner Blaser
6. erw. Auflage,
248 Seiten,
180 Abbildungen
ISBN 3-7643-5619-7
deutsch / englisch

Jean Nouvel
Olivier Boissière
208 Seiten,
300 Abbildungen
ISBN 3-7643-5356-2
deutsch / englisch

Andrea Palladio
Die vier Bücher zur Architektur
A. Beyer und U. Schütte
4., überarbeitete Auflage.
472 Seiten
ISBN 3-7643-5561-1

Alvaro Siza
Peter Testa
192 Seiten,
300 Abbildungen
ISBN 3-7643-5598-0
deutsch / englisch

Luigi Snozzi
Claude Lichtenstein
208 Seiten,
400 Abbildungen
ISBN 3-7643-5439-9
deutsch / englisch

**James Stirling/
Michael Wilford**
Robert Maxwell
208 Seiten,
223 Abbildungen
ISBN 3-7643-5291-4
deutsch / englisch

Louis Henry Sullivan
Hans Frei
176 Seiten,
208 Abbildungen
ISBN 3-7643-5574-3
deutsch / englisch

Oswald Mathias Ungers
Martin Kieren
256 Seiten,
406 Abbildungen
ISBN 3-7643-5585-9
deutsch / englisch